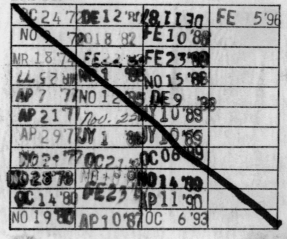

American Theories of Federalism

Walter Hartwell Bennett

AMERICAN
THEORIES
of
FEDERALISM

University of Alabama Press
University, Alabama

To My Mother

Contents

Preface

THE SIGNIFICANT ROLE WHICH THE THEORY OF FEDER-
alism has played in the shaping of the political institutions of
the United States and in the formation of its public policy makes
it of primary interest to students of American history and
American government. Consequently, it has been dealt with in
various ways in works by American authors. When it has been
given special treatment, however, attention has been focused
usually on comparatively brief periods of history or on opinions of the United States Supreme Court in cases relating to the
federal distribution of powers under the United States Constitution. American authors have not endeavored to deal with
the history of the theory in its entirety in any of their published works. Perhaps the most extensive treatment in print is
found in *The Problem of Federalism*, by the Japanese scholar
Sobei Mogi. This work draws attention to most of the important treatises between 1787 and the early part of the twentieth
century in which the character of the union under the Constitution is a major subject of discussion; but the book has
barely tapped the large quantity of polemical writings and
public documentary materials which relate to American federalism.

The present study does not purport to deal with all phases of
American theorizing about federal systems of government;
but it is an attempt to analyze in detail the different conceptions of federal union or federal government which Americans have from time to time advanced and to indicate the im-

portance which these conceptions have had in political controversy. In only an incidental fashion have ideas relating to the desirability of federalism or to the advantages or disadvantages of this or that federal form been taken into account. The study concentrates, instead, on the legal aspects of federalism as these aspects have been viewed by American constitutional theorists. It has necessarily involved a great deal of delving in the realm of legal metaphysics, since it was common until 1900 for Americans to approach federalism from the point of view of a priori notions of the nature of the state and its sovereignty.

In determining the scope of the study, the term "federal" has been given a broader meaning than it has often had—a meaning broad enough for the term to be used as a label in referring to any political system in which there is a constitutional distribution of powers between provincial governments and a common central authority. Such a distribution is conceived by the author to be the essence of federalism. It is the one feature that has been common to all of the political systems to which the term federal has been applied in American literature.

My interest in this subject began some years ago when I prepared a thesis for the doctorate at Duke University on American concepts of federalism from the colonial period to 1900. Portions of this thesis have been incorporated, with substantial modifications, in this book.

For financial support for the study, I am principally indebted to the Research Committee of the University of Alabama. Other assistance, in the form of grants or research and clerical aid, has been supplied by the Social Science Research Council and the Bureau of Public Administration of the University of Alabama.

My indebtedness to scholars whose works I have consulted is at least partially indicated by the footnote references. However, I must record my thanks to friends and associates who have given me assistance and encouragement. I owe special thanks to Dr. R. Taylor Cole, Provost of Duke University, who counseled me in my early research efforts on federalism and has since given me helpful advice. Dr. Leslie W. Dunbar, Executive Director of the Southern Regional Council, Atlanta, and my colleague Professor Robert B. Highsaw of the University of Alabama, have both read the manuscript and made comments that were helpful in revising it. Dr. Ralph E. Purcell, at present visiting professor at The George Washington University, read six of the chapters and by his suggestions assisted me in clarifying my thoughts on a number of points. I am grateful to Mrs. Doris Albright, former Secretary of the Department of Political Science of the University of Alabama, for seeing that I was provided with clerical assistance, and to Mrs. Eunice H. Payne and Mrs. Nancy H. Seebeck of the University of Alabama Press for the patience and skill demonstrated by their editing of the manuscript for publication. Finally, I am indebted to my wife, Maxine Purcell Bennett, who has helped me with many of the wearisome tasks which the study has entailed.

For uniformity, capitalization in the text has been normalized. In certain passages quoted from the earlier documents, spelling has been modernized for clarity.

WALTER H. BENNETT

University of Alabama
October, 1963

American Theories of Federalism

The fundamental principle of the Revolution was, that the colonies were co-ordinate members with each other, and with Great Britain, of an empire, united by a common executive sovereign, but not united by any common legislative sovereign. The legislative power was maintained to be as complete in each American parliament, as in the British parliament. And the royal prerogative was in force in each colony, by virtue of its acknowledging the king for its executive magistrate as it was in Great Britain, by virtue of a like acknowledgment there. A denial of these principles by Great Britain, and the assertion of them by America, produced the Revolution.

—From James Madison's Legislative Committee Report of 1800 defending the position taken by the Virginia legislature in adopting the Virginia Resolutions of 1798. *Debates in the Several State Conventions on the Adoption of the Federal Constitution*, ed. Jonathan Elliot, 2nd edition (1836), IV, 589.

(1)

The Federalized Empire

AMERICAN THEORIZING ABOUT FEDERAL GOVERNMENT began in the colonial era, during which there was frequent speculation about the nature of the British Empire. It is true that the Empire as it existed in the seventeenth and eighteenth centuries differed from most political systems to which the label "federal" has been applied. It differed from such systems in not being a union that had been deliberately created by bringing together a number of political communities previously separated from one another. The American colonies belonging to the Empire had been planted one by one by the mother country, and most present-day students of American colonial history would probably agree that whatever autonomy the colonies enjoyed was possessed by them as a result of devolution from the center. Nevertheless, this autonomy was real, and there were those in these two centuries who thought of it as existing as a matter of constitutional right— who, in other words, thought of the Empire, not as a unitary state but as a composite of several political entities each supreme in its own sphere as defined by the Empire's basic law.[1] Both near the beginning and near the end of the colonial

---

[1] Definitely one of the best treatments concerning the division of authority between the colonies and the mother country is contained in Charles H. McIlwain's *The American Revolution: A Constitutional Interpretation* (New York, 1923). Professor McIlwain is one of several American scholars who have suggested that the pattern of federalism under the United States Constitution is to be traced in part to the experience of the colonies in dealing with the mother country. For some recent statements

era there were controversies over the corporate rights of the colonies. The first concerned specifically the relationship of the Massachusetts Bay Colony to England, and the American participants were leaders in this Colony. The second was far more general, since it was a part of the great controversy with England which began shortly after the passage by Parliament of the Stamp Act of 1765 and ended with the independence of the colonies. It is with the arguments set forth by colonial leaders and relating to the corporate rights of the colonies that this chapter will deal.

Conception of the British Empire in Early Massachusetts

In its early history the Massachusetts Bay Colony acted as if it were an almost completely self-governing community. So extreme were the claims of its stubborn Puritan leaders for self-government that it is sometimes difficult to see in their statements even an admission of a federal connection with the mother country. However, they did at all times acknowledge a connection. They professed to be loyal to the king, and, while there is some evidence to the contrary, they presumably recognized some obligation to respect regulations laid down under the king's prerogative. Their theory of the relation of the Colony to Parliament varied from an acknowledged subordination to Parliament to the view that Parliament had no authority whatever over the Colony.

A brief passage in John Winthrop's *Journal* for the year 1641 indicates that the principal leaders of the Colony believed at that date that the Colony was only loosely joined to the mother country through allegiance to the king. "Friends" in England had suggested that the colonists send over agents

of this thesis see his essay, "The Historical Background of Federal Government," in the symposium *Federalism as a Democratic Process,* by Roscoe Pound, Charles H. McIlwain, and Roy F. Nichols (New Brunswick, 1942), and Robert Livingston Schuyler, "British Imperial Theory and American Territorial Policy—A Suggested Relationship," *Proceedings of the American Philosophical Society,* XCVII, No. 4 (September, 1953), 317-31.

"to solicit" for them in Parliament, pointing out that the king now allowed greater liberty than formerly to Parliament, and that there was therefore much to be gained if the agents were sent. The matter was considered in the Colony, but it was decided not to send the agents. According to Winthrop, the colonial leaders took the position that sending them would mean submission to the protection of Parliament and subjection to Parliamentary legislation.[2] This, at least, would seem to imply that any rights to governmental authority over the Colony were considered to be rights that belonged either to the king's prerogative or to the local colonial organs.[3]

Five years later, church elders in the Massachusetts Bay Colony were asked to prepare a report on the relation of the Colony to England. As a preliminary, the magistrates of the Colony severally spoke their minds in order to afford the elders the benefit of the magistrates' opinions. According to Winthrop, some of the magistrates believed the government of the Colony to be "subordinate" to Parliament, and others, while conceding that "allegiance and subjection" were owed to Parliament, were of the opinion that the Charter of the Colony conferred "absolute power" of government. The latter recognized that the "Commonwealth" of Massachusetts was "founded" on the power of England, and that on "great occasions" it depended upon England for advice and counsel. In respect to matters of government, however, they considered the Colony to be independent of England, regarding the position of the Colony in the Empire as similar to that of Normandy and Gascony when these provinces had been "dependent" upon the Crown of France but had yet been "independent" of France insofar as matters of government were concerned. Further analogies were believed to be

[2] *Winthrop's Journal*, ed. J. K. Hosmer (New York, 1908), II, 24.
[3] Governor Jonathan Trumbull of Connecticut, 138 years later, cited this incident as a precedent for opposing Parliamentary control over the colonies. See letter of Governor Trumbull to Baron J. D. Vander Capellan, *Collections of the Massachusetts Historical Society*, 1st Ser., VI, 154–85, at pp. 155-56.

afforded by Burgundy and Flanders, and the Hanse towns of Germany. While the Hanse towns were recognized as having been subject to the Imperial Chamber of the "empire" in some "great and general causes," it was pointed out that they were represented by deputies when such causes were under consideration.[4]

In their report, the Massachusetts elders conceded that "allegiance and fidelity" were owed to England and that the Colony was dependent upon England for protection. On the other hand, they claimed that the Charter of the Colony conferred upon the Colony full powers of choosing all colonial officers and of making "full and final determination of all cases in the administration of justice." There could be no appeal to England from the colonial courts.[5]

After 1660 Massachusetts bitterly protested against the British navigation acts. On one occasion the General Court asserted that "according to the usual sayings of the learned in law," the laws of England were bounded within the four seas and did not reach America. Since the king's subjects in America were not represented in Parliament, they had not looked upon themselves as subject to the Parliamentary acts of trade. The General Court acknowledged a "relative allegiance" to the king and explained that it had by special enactment made the navigation acts effective in the Colony as soon as it had been understood that the king had wished those acts to be in force there. But the General Court added that the navigation acts could not in the absence of colonial approval have been applied in the Colony "without invading the liberties and properties of the subject."[6]

Edward Randolph, a British agent in America, made numerous reports to the home government in which he devoted space to the attitude of Massachusetts. In one report he said

[4] *Winthrop's Journal*, II, 290-91.   [5] *Ibid.*, II, 294.
[6] *Records of the Governor and Company of the Massachusetts Bay*, ed. Nathaniel Shurtleff (Boston), V, 200. Hereinafter cited as *Records of Massachusetts Bay*.

that the governor of the Colony had declared to him that "laws made by the king and Parliament oblige them in nothing but what consists with the interest of New England." He quoted the governor as having said that the colonial Charter gave Massachusetts the right to make laws "not repugnant to the laws of England." According to Randolph, the governor took the position that the Colony alone could decide matters of difference between itself and the mother country. Some of the people in the Colony, said Randolph, had even asserted that the king could not retrench the liberties which he had extended to them.[7]

Randolph was actually imprisoned in New England. He later declared that he had made himself obnoxious by his attempt as collector of customs in 1679 to enforce observance of the navigation acts. The colonial officials, he said, "openly denied and opposed" his commission. They denied that the acts of trade or any other law of England had any legal force in the Colony unless ratified by the General Court. Despite admonitions of the king and others, the illegal trade had continued.[8]

In a report to "several heads of inquiry" in 1676, Randolph noted that it was considered a breach of privilege in Massachusetts to urge observance of the laws of England. He cited a number of laws in Massachusetts which he held to be contrary to the laws of England. Further, he noted that the only oaths taken in the Colony were "those of fidelity to the government." Oaths of allegiance to the king, he said, were not taken.[9]

A report of the Lords of Trade and Plantations, dated February 6, 1677, also took cognizance of the opposition of New England to the acts of trade. It was explained in the report that the Lords had prepared rules "for passes to all ships

[7] Edward Randolph to Secretary Coventry, 1676, *Calendar of State Papers*, Colonial Ser., America and West Indies, IX, 407.
[8] *The Andros Tracts* (Boston, 1869), II, 184.
[9] *Calendar of State Papers*, IX, 464.

trading to and from England and settled the rules to Ireland, Jersey, Guernsey, and Tangier," but that no rules had been framed for New England. It was pointed out that the people of New England, instead of complying with the acts of trade, took the liberty of trading where they pleased. Furthermore, the report warned that some understanding should be arrived at concerning "the degrees of dependence that government will acknowledge to His Majesty."[10]

A pamphlet published in 1689 and entitled *A Short Discourse* condemned Massachusetts for its attitude of independence. The author cited a Massachusetts law of 1663 calling upon the inhabitants of the Colony to observe one of the British acts of trade as plain evidence that the Colony considered the laws of England to have no force in the Colony until ratified by the General Court. He noted, moreover, that the Massachusetts "Law Book" of 1672 stipulated that no law should be submitted to in the Colony unless it had been adopted by the General Court.[11]

Leaders of early Massachusetts never tired of calling attention to that portion of the Colony's Charter which said in effect that the privileges conferred on the colonists were granted in perpetuity. Thus, a petition of the Massachusetts General Court to Charles II in 1664 declared:

> We shall not largely repeat how that the first undertakers for this plantation, having by considerable sums purchased the right thereof, granted to the counsel established at Plymouth by King James, your royal grandfather, did after obtain a patent given & confirmed to themselves by your royal father, King Charles the First, wherein is granted unto them, their heirs, assigns, & associates forever, not only absolute use & propriety of the tract of land therein mentioned, but also full & absolute power of governing all the people of this place, by men chosen from among themselves, & according to such laws as they shall from time to time see meet to make and establish, being not repugnant to the

[10] *Ibid.*, X, 15-16.
[11] *The Andros Tracts*, II, 138-39.

laws of England, (they paying only the fifth part of the ore of
gold and silver that shall here be found for & in respect of all
duties, demands, exactions, & services whatsoever). . . .[12]

The Pre-Revolutionary Era

When the British Parliament sought by the Stamp Act in
1765 to enter the field of "internal taxation" in the colonies,
speculation over the relation of the colonies to the mother
country became general. The Stamp tax was repealed the year
after its enactment, but the very act by which Parliament
repealed the tax included a proviso in which it was asserted
that Parliament had the right to legislate for the colonies in
all matters whatsoever.

This position of Parliament was defended both in England
and in America by invoking the conception of absolute and
indivisible sovereignty commonly attributed to the sixteenth-
century Frenchman Jean Bodin.[13] William Bollan, who served
in England for many years as an agent for the colony of Massachusetts, argued in his pamphlet, *A Succinct View of the
Origin of Our Colonies* (1766), that the nature of human
government made necessary the existence and occasional exercise in every state of "a supreme legislative jurisdiction."
For the British Empire this jurisdiction was vested in Parliament. The colonies, because of "their situation, nature, and
necessary political existence," possessed "subordinate powers
of legislation"; but "the sole *summum imperium* of the Brit-

[12] *Records of Massachusetts Bay*, IV, Pt. II, 129.
[13] In his *Six livres de la république*, first published in 1576, Bodin defined
sovereignty as "the most high, absolute, and perpetuall power over the
citizens and subjects in a commonweale." This power was unrestrained
by positive law and was incapable of division. But Bodin did not apply
his definition strictly; instead, he eventually concluded that there were in
a state certain *leges imperii*, or laws concerning the form of government,
which the sovereign was obligated to observe. See the *Six Bookes of a
Commonweale*, English translation of the *République* by Richard Knolles
(London, 1606; facsimile reprint corrected and supplemented by a new
comparison with the French and Latin texts, ed. Kenneth Douglas Mc-
Rae, Cambridge, Mass., 1962), Book I, Chaps. 8 & 10, passim; Book II,
Chap. 1, passim.

ish Parliament" remained "firm, immutable and universal."[14]

In his letters of "Massachusettensis," published in the Boston *Gazette* in 1774 and 1775, the Boston lawyer Daniel Leonard declared that it would be the height of political absurdity for two supreme and independent authorities to exist within the same state. The analogy between the political and the human body was great. "Two independent authorities in a state would be like two distinct principles of volition and action in the human body, dissenting, opposing, and destroying each other." If the colonies were a part of the British Empire, they must be subject to Parliament, which possessed the supreme power of the Empire. This was true notwithstanding the fact that each of the colonies enjoyed by delegation or grant legislative and executive powers of its own in matters of internal police. The powers enjoyed by a colony were necessarily subject "to the checks, control and regulation of the supreme authority."[15]

The same doctrine was elaborated upon by Dr. Samuel Johnson in his *Taxation No Tyranny* (1775).

> In sovereignty there are no gradations. There may be limited royalty; there may be limited consulship; but there can be no limited government. There must, in every society, be some power or other from which there is no appeal; which admits of no restrictions; which pervades the whole mass of the community; regulates and adjusts all subordination; enacts laws and repeals them; erects or annuls judicatures; extends or contracts privileges; exempt itself from question or control; and bounded only by physical necessity.
>
> By this power, wherever it subsists, all legislation and jurisdiction is animated and maintained. From this all legal rights are emanations; which, whether equitably or not, may be legally recalled. It is not infallible, for it may do wrong, but it is irresistible,

[14] William Bollan, *A Succinct View of the Origin of Our Colonies* (London, 1766), p. 10.
[15] Massachusettensis, pseud. of Daniel Leonard, *The Present Political State of the Province of Massachusetts Bay in General, and the Town of Boston, in Particular* (New York, 1775), pp. 7, 56.

for it can be resisted only by rebellion—by an act which makes it questionable what shall be thenceforward the supreme power.[16]

An English colony was defined by Johnson as a number of persons to whom the king had given a charter permitting them to settle in some distant country and enabling them to exist as a corporation, enjoying such powers as the charter granted. The colony made laws for itself as a corporation, but as a corporation subsisting by grant from higher authority. To the control of the higher authority the colony continued to be subject.[17]

Governor Thomas Hutchinson appealed to the sovereignty doctrine in his disputes with the General Court of Massachusetts in the 1770's. He professed to know of no line that could be drawn between the supreme authority of Parliament and the total independence of the colonies. When members of the General Court took the position that the British Empire was an example of two powers, each supreme in a particular legislative sphere, and that such powers were not incompatible, Hutchinson explained that a supreme power was essential in all governments, that another power with the name of subordinate and with the right to withstand or control the supreme in some particulars was an absurdity. He ventured to add that no sensible writer on government had ever denied what he asserted.[18]

As a general rule, those Americans who opposed the extreme Parliamentary position did not discuss the nature of sovereignty, although they did occasionally deal with the subject when it was raised by supporters of Parliamentary control over the colonies.[19] Their appeal was mainly to the

[16] Samuel Johnson, *Taxation No Tyranny*, reprinted in *American Archives*, ed. Peter Force, 4th Ser., Vol. I, cols. 1431-49, at col. 1436.
[17] *Idem.*
[18] Quoted in V. L. Parrington, *Main Currents in American Thought* (New York, 1927), I, 203.
[19] An attack on the doctrine of absolute and indivisible sovereignty was contained in a pamphlet which has been attributed to Benjamin Franklin and which was intended as an answer to Dr. Samuel Johnson's *Taxation*

constitutional law of the British Empire and to abstract principles of natural law and contract. Conceptions of the Empire varied among them as they had among the early leaders of Massachusetts. Some virtually conceded that the colonies were obligated to respect Parliamentary enactments on any matter which could reasonably be defined as falling within the category of external affairs while holding at the same time that the colonial assemblies possessed exclusive legislative jurisdiction over all matters of internal policy. Others were explicit in arguing that the colonies were not annexed to the realm of Great Britain, that allegiance was due from the inhabitants of the colonies to the person entitled to wear the British Crown, not to the British Kingdom. In other words, the Empire was a personal union of co-ordinate commonwealths, the commonwealths in America being on a plane of exact legal equality with the one in England. All, or nearly all, recognized as valid the British acts of trade and were apparently ready to concede that the intercolonial and foreign commerce of the colonies was not a proper subject for legislation by the colonial legislatures. On the question of the basis of the authority to regulate the trade of the colonies, however, there was no unanimity of opinion. Some, while protesting against the interference of Parliament in internal affairs, appear to have regarded the authority of Parliament to regulate trade as inherent in the central legislative body of the Empire. Others, holding the legislative sovereignty of the colonies to be virtually complete, maintained that the authority of Parliament to regulate the trade of the colonies was

---

No Tyranny. The author declared that the notion of an absolute supremacy in government was "an ignorant, false, and ignominious idea, when adopted by an Englishman and applied to the English Constitution." However much the theory might be true elsewhere, it was not the Constitution of England. The supremacy for which Dr. Johnson contended had been the "cant of prerogative times," and was now preached up "to exist in any part of the legislative authority" in which it was desired to have it lodged. *Tyranny Unmasked: An Answer to Taxation No Tyranny* (London, 1775), pp. 50 ff.

based upon the tacit consent of the colonies. Finally, there were those who regarded this authority as belonging neither to Parliament nor to the colonial assemblies, but rather to the king's prerogative. An effort will be made here to analyze the conceptions of the Empire held by some of the principal opponents of unlimited Parliamentary control.

In his *The Rights of the Colonies Examined* (1765), Stephen Hopkins represented the British Empire as a composite state of many separate governments, according to each government a sphere of authority. Holding that in such a state no single part had the right to legislate for or to tax a lesser part, he argued that all laws and taxes placed upon the whole should be enacted by the whole. To illustrate, he cited the example of the Holy Roman Empire. Here, he observed, was an empire consisting of many states, some strong and some weak, where the stronger states did not legislate for or tax the weaker states. Instead of imperial control being exercised by one of the states of the empire, it was exercised by a diet consisting "of representatives of the whole body."[20]

Hopkins appears to have been half inclined to advocate a reorganization of Parliament in order to allow "the separate kingdoms and distant colonies" to be represented whenever matters affecting the Empire as a whole were being considered. In effect, however, he conceded that Parliament as it was already constituted could constitutionally legislate on any subject which concerned "the proper interest and fit government of the whole common-wealth." He regarded the commerce of the Empire as a subject which should be regulated by Parliament, and he thought that money and credit might also be found to be proper subjects of Parliamentary enactments.[21]

In his essay entitled *An Inquiry into the Rights of the British Colonies* (1766), Richard Bland defended the proposi-

---

[20] Stephen Hopkins, *The Rights of the Colonies Examined* (Providence, 1765), pp. 19-20.
[21] *Ibid.*, p. 10.

tion that the colonies were "united" to the "original kingdom" in respect to their "*external* polity" and that they were "independent" in respect to their "*internal* government." Conceding that there was a "degree" of dependence of the colonies on the British Parliament, he argued that in British practice the colonists had always been treated as distinct from the people of Great Britain. He pointed out that the king had not disdained to deal with the Colony of Virginia through its own legislature rather than through the Parliament of Great Britain, that when a permanent revenue for the Colony had been contemplated, the king had appealed, not to Parliament, but to the General Assembly of the Colony. The British government had regarded the colonists as a distinct people "in every instance of Parliamentary legislation," said Bland. Moreover, the Lords of the Privy Council had held that acts of Parliament that did not name the foreign plantations did not apply to those plantations.[22]

To support his theory that the colonies were a distinct people and partially independent of the sovereignty of Great Britain, Bland employed ideas of natural rights and of contract. He argued that the law of nature gave men a right to renounce the sovereignty of the state where they had lived and to move to another country. It was their privilege to withdraw whenever they found that membership in the original society was no longer conducive to their happiness. In the new country they recovered their "natural freedom and independence," and could, if they wished, form a new and independent state. On the other hand, they could, if they chose, proceed on the basis of a new compact with their original sovereign. If they did this, the compact would constitute a binding agreement between the parties and would be the "Magna Charta" of the new government.[23]

The somewhat more moderate John Dickinson did not

---

[22] Richard Bland, *An Inquiry into the Rights of the British Colonies,* ed. E. G. Swem (Richmond, 1922), pp. 12, 20.
[23] *Ibid.,* pp. 10, 14.

regard such terms as "distinct people" and "distinct states" as descriptive of the legal status of the colonies. The colonies were to be looked upon as "parts of a whole." In his *Letters from a Farmer*, first published in 1767 and 1768, Dickinson readily accepted the view that the British Parliament, without representation from the colonies, had the power to regulate the foreign commerce of the colonies, holding that there necessarily existed somewhere in the Empire a power "to preside, and preserve the connection in due order."[24] But in consideration for the powers exercised over the colonies by the mother country she had compensated them by extending to them "a communication of her rights in general." She had especially extended to them the right of not having their property disposed of by anyone but themselves.[25]

Dickinson drew a sharp distinction between duties imposed for the purpose of regulating colonial trade and taxes imposed on the colonists by Parliament for revenue purposes. The former, he said, represented a legitimate exercise of Parliamentary power, while the taxes were an unconstitutional innovation.[26] That it was possible for the "supremacy" of Great Britain to exist without Parliament's having the right to levy taxes for revenue purposes in the colonies Dickinson held to have been proven by the history of the British settlements in America. He claimed that in a period of more than 150 years Parliament had never attempted to raise revenue in the colonies by taxation.[27]

None of the writers of the decade immediately preceding the American Revolution examined more thoroughly than did John Adams the subject of the constitutional status of the

---

[24] John Dickinson, *Letters from a Farmer in Pennsylvania* (New York, 1903), p. 13.   [25] *Ibid.*, p. 51.

[26] *Ibid.*, pp. 18-19. This distinction between the power to tax for the purpose of regulating trade and the power to tax for revenue was made by Daniel Dulany in 1765. See Dulany's *Considerations on the Propriety of Imposing Taxes in the British Colonies, for the Purpose of Raising a Revenue, by Act of Parliament* (North America, 1765), p. 29.

[27] Dickinson, pp. 47 ff.

colonies as members of the British Empire. In his letters of "Novanglus," which were meant to answer the propositions advanced by Daniel Leonard, Adams examined with painstaking care the legal precedents tending to show that the colonial legislatures had supreme legislative power over the colonies. According to him, any right of Parliament to regulate the foreign and intercolonial trade of the colonies was based solely on the consent of the colonies as political communities. The colonies had agreed for Parliament to regulate the colonial trade because of considerations of necessity. The power over trade had been allowed to Parliament rather than to some other British legislature because Parliament was the most "powerful" of the several legislatures. By "express consent" the colonies had contracted to observe a "Navigation Act," and by "implied consent, by long usage and uninterrupted acquiescence," they had submitted to the other acts of trade. The result, according to Adams, was comparable to "a treaty of commerce," by which "those distinct states" were bound "in perpetual league and amity."[28]

Adams denied that the colonies were annexed to the realm of Great Britain, holding that such annexation would necessitate action both by the British Parliament and by the colonial assemblies. If the king had granted the Charter of Massachusetts as "King of England, Scotland, France and Ireland," it was as reasonable to argue that America was to be governed by the Irish Parliament as to argue that it was to be governed by the English Parliament. Moreover, it didn't matter if the Charter was granted under the Great Seal of England, for the Great Seal "runneth not out of the realm." The truth was that the realm of Great Britain was not the only realm within the British Empire. The Empire contained a large number of realms, for Ireland, Massachusetts, New York, and Pennsylvania were all distinct realms, "as much as England or Scot-

[28] John Adams, "Novanglus," *The Works of John Adams,* ed. C. F. Adams (Boston, 1850-56), IV, 49, 99-100, 105, 113-14.

land ever were [sic]." There was no absurdity in the king's being king of Massachusetts, king of Rhode Island, and king of Connecticut.[29]

The principles of feudal law were examined by Adams to prove that allegiance to the Crown did not mean allegiance to the realm of Great Britain or subjection to the British Parliament. He pointed out that the oath of fealty taken under the feudal law by a vassal or tenant was "nearly in the very words of the ancient oath of allegiance." "Neither fealty, allegiance, or the oath of either implied anything about laws, parliaments, lords, or commons."[30]

> The word *crown*, like the word *throne*, is used in various figurative senses; sometimes it means the kingly office, the head of the commonwealth; but it does not always mean the political capacity of the king; much less does it include in the idea of it, lords and commons. It may as well be pretended that the House of Commons includes or implies a king. Nay, it may as well be pretended that the mace includes the three branches of the legislature.
>
> By the feudal law, a person or a country might be subject to a king, a feudal sovereign, three several ways.
>
> 1. It might be subject to his person; and in this case it would continue so subject, let him be where he would, in his dominions or without. 2. To his crown; and in this case subjection was due to whatever person or family wore that crown, and would follow it, whatever revolutions it underwent. 3. To his crown and realm of state; and in this case it was incorporated as one body with the principal kingdom; and if that was bound by a parliament, diet, or cortes, so was the other.
>
> It is humbly conceived, that the subjection of the colonies by compact and law, is of the second sort.[31]

Adams conceived of the relation between the king and his American subjects in terms of a series of original contracts. In the charter colonies the charters themselves were concrete

---

[29] *Ibid.*, IV, 114-15, 123-24, 174-75.   [30] *Ibid.*, IV, 145.
[31] *Ibid.*, IV, 140.

embodiments of such contracts, while in the royal colonies the contracts found expression in commissions to the royal governors. After the Revolution of 1688 in England, the people of Massachusetts had made "an original express contract with King William," just as had the people of England.[32]

Adams agreed with Leonard's contention that two supreme and independent authorities could not exist in the same state, assuming that this doctrine supported his own contention that the colonial legislatures were the supreme authorities in the colonies. According to Adams, the term "state" was applicable to a part of the Empire, but not to the Empire itself. It is obvious, however, that supremacy did not mean the same thing to him as it did to Leonard. Adams was willing to concede to Parliament "an authority supreme and sovereign over the ocean," holding that there was no inconsistency in claiming "absolute independence" for the colonies in all internal concerns while conceding their "absolute dependence" in respect to external commerce. It was not true that there was no medium between absolute independence and subjection. The "banks of the ocean, or low water mark," constituted a line fairly drawn between the rights of Great Britain and the rights of the colonies.[33]

James Wilson was fully in accord with the view that the American colonies were not legally annexed to the realm of Great Britain. Like Adams, Wilson held that the real link of the colonies to the mother country was the king. Wilson argued in effect that such expressions as "dependence on Great Britain" and "within the allegiance of England," all in common usage, ought to have reference to the relation between the colonial people and the king, that the expressions

[32] *Ibid.*, IV, 114 ff. In 1818 Adams observed that the charter issued by James I to the London Company was "more like a treaty between independent sovereigns than like a charter or grant of privileges from a sovereign to his subjects." Letter of Adams to William Tudor in *ibid.*, X, 359.
[33] *Ibid.*, IV, 105 ff.

had nothing to do with any relation between the colonial people and the Kingdom of England.[34]

> There is another, and a much more reasonable meaning, which may be intended by the dependence of the colonies on Great-Britain. The phrase may be used to denote the obedience and loyalty, which the colonists owe to the *kings* of Great-Britain. If it should be alleged, that this cannot be the meaning of the expression, because it is applied to the *kingdom,* and not to the *king,* I give the same answer that my Lord Bacon gave to those who said that allegiance related to the Kingdom and not to the king; because in the statutes there are these words—"born within the allegiance of *England*"—and again—"born without the allegiance of England." "There is no trope of speech more familiar," says he, "than to use the place of addition for the person. So we say commonly, the line of York, or the line of Lancaster, for the lines of the duke of York, or the duke of Lancaster. So we say the possessions of Somerset or Warwick, intending the possessions of the dukes of Somerset, or earls of Warwick. And in the very same manner, the statute speaks, allegiance of England, for allegiance of the king of England."[35]

Wilson held that the early settlers and the most eminent of the lawyers of seventeenth-century England had understood "dependence" in this sense. He noted that it nowhere appeared that the early settlers considered themselves to be represented in the English Parliament or subject to the laws of that body, although they did consider themselves to be subjects of the king.

> They took possession of the country in the *king's* name: they treated, or made war with the Indians by *his* authority: they held the lands under *his* grants, and paid *him* the rents reserved upon them: they established governments under the sanction of *his* prerogative, or by virtue of *his* charters:—no application for those purposes was made to the Parliament: no ratification of the

---

[34] James Wilson, *Works,* ed. James DeWitt Andrews (Chicago, 1896), II, 534 ff.
[35] *Ibid.,* II, 536-37.

charters or letters patent was solicited from that assembly, as is usual in England with regard to grants and franchises of much less importance.[36]

According to Wilson, the king and not Parliament was legally authorized to direct and manage the "great machine of government" of the Empire. Among the specific functions of the king were those of making war, forming alliances, and concluding peace. By his prerogative the king could regulate trade within the Empire, and foreign commerce was regulated by treaties between the king and foreign nations. The king appointed executive officers of government, the performance of which function provided him with an opportunity to check "every jarring movement in the administration." He possessed a veto over the various legislatures of the Empire, and through the use of this veto he could prevent conflicts between the enactments of the legislatures.[37]

A prerogative in the king to regulate trade Wilson regarded as perfectly consistent with law. He recognized that many authorities had held that the king could not lay impositions upon or prohibit trade nor confine it to monopolists; but he noted that none of the authorities whom he had consulted had gone any further. Many of them, he observed, had seemed to imply that the king had power to regulate trade when the power was exercised for the public good.[38]

While Wilson regarded the king as the sole authority within the Empire for "general" imperial functions, he clearly did not assume that the king's prerogative was unlimited. To prove that it was limited he argued from ideas of divine and natural rights and compact. He held that since the Revolution of 1688 it was the easiest thing imaginable to prove the existence of a compact in the "British" Constitution. While the compact had often been broken, it also had often been renewed and confirmed, and it still bound the king in the same sense that it bound the meanest subject. It limited the king

[36] *Ibid.*, II, 537.   [37] *Ibid.*, II, 541-42.
[38] *Ibid.*, II, 542 and note.

both in respect to what he did pursuant to law and in respect to what he did without special provision of law but on the authority of his own prerogative. In the former case, the king was obliged to respect the limitations specified in the law, while in the latter, his procedure should be "conducted by the best rules of discretion, agreeably to the general spirit of the laws, and subserviently to their ultimate end—the interests and happiness of his subjects."[39] On the basis of this reasoning, Wilson concluded that the king had no right to alter the Charter of Massachusetts. He held that the legislature of the Colony would itself have to give its consent before any change in the Colony's Charter could legally be made.[40]

Holding that the people were the source of all governmental authority, Wilson argued that the same powers which the House of Commons derived from its constituents were entrusted by the inhabitants of the colonies to their assemblies. The American assemblies were authorized to propose and assent to laws for the government of their electors just as Parliament was authorized to propose and assent to laws for the government of the inhabitants of Great Britain.[41]

Wilson noted that there was a doctrine to the effect that there existed in every state a "supreme, irresistible, absolute, uncontrolled authority," and that some held that this authority had been vested by the British Constitution in the king, lords, and commons. He did not specifically indicate what he thought of this theory of sovereignty, but he went on to argue that no one had a right to exercise authority over another without the other's consent. He also insisted at this point that it was a rule of nature that government should endeavor to insure and increase the happiness of the governed and that this rule must control every political maxim.[42]

---

[39] *Ibid.*, II, 558.   [40] *Ibid.*, II, 558-59.
[41] James Wilson, "An Address to the Inhabitants of the Colonies," *Selected Political Essays of James Wilson*, ed. R. G. Adams (New York, 1930), pp. 103-21, at p. 106.
[42] Wilson, *Works*, II, 506-08.

Evidently, in 1754, Benjamin Franklin understood Parliament to possess supreme legislative authority over the whole of the British Empire. At least he took the position in that year that Parliament was competent to give legal effect to the Albany plan of union of which he was one of the architects.[43] However, he was one of those who opposed Parliamentary supremacy following the passage of the Stamp Act. During the controversy over this Act, he declared that the authority of Parliament was confined to the realm of Great Britain. The "sovereignty of the Crown" over the colonies he understood, but not the "sovereignty of the British Legislature" over the colonies.[44] The members of the British legislature were undoubtedly proper judges of what concerned the welfare of Great Britain, but the American legislators were proper judges for what concerned the "American states."[45] It was no part of the "original constitution" of the colonies for them to have to submit to acts of Parliament. Former British kings had governed their colonies as they had governed their dominions in France, i.e., without the participation of Parliament. Nor had Parliament, until the "great Rebellion," ever presumed to interfere with the "prerogative" by which the colonies were governed.[46]

Admitting the legality of the royal veto over the colonial assemblies, Franklin took the position that the king could not change laws passed in the colonies once the royal assent was given. He held that instructions to the royal governors were not necessarily the law of the land.[47] He suggested, moreover, that there were times when a dissolution of a colonial assembly would be a violation of common right and a breach of the British Constitution.[48]

The general conception of the British Empire which ap-

---

[43] See Chap. II of this work.
[44] Benjamin Franklin, *Writings*, ed. A. H. Smyth (London, 1907), X, 235, 236.
[45] *Ibid.*, X, 237.
[46] *Ibid.*, V, 238.
[47] *Ibid.*, I, 434-35; V, 359.
[48] *Ibid.*, VI, 210-11.

pears in the writings of Adams, Wilson, and Franklin in the pre-Revolutionary decade was also present in Thomas Jefferson's *Summary View of the Rights of British America* (1774). Jefferson argued that each of the "states" of the Empire possessed within itself the sovereign powers of legislation, holding that every society must at all times possess such powers "from the nature of things." The functions of legislation were exercised by representative bodies as long as such bodies existed, and, in the event of the dissolution of such bodies, the right to legislate reverted to the people, to be exercised in such manner as the people thought proper. Actually each state of the Empire had its own independent legislature which had sole power, while in existence, to legislate for the people whom it represented.[49] However, one of the legislatures had usurped powers belonging to the others.[50]

The king, according to Jefferson, was supposed to be the "chief magistrate" and the "mediatory power" in the Empire. The king was the executive officer of each state of the Empire, but he was to administer the laws of a particular state in that state only. Thus, it was unlawful for him to send armed troops to America without the consent of the colonial legislatures. Every state of the Empire had the right to judge for itself the number of armed men it could safely trust within its limits. Moreover, each state had the right to pass upon the composition of the troops and upon the restrictions under which they were to be placed.[51]

The king had the role of mediating between the several legislatures of the Empire, and this duty ought to be discharged by the use of his power to veto acts passed by the several legislatures. In Great Britain he had for a long time "modestly declined" to use this power, but the addition of new states to the Empire now made it necessary to resume the use of the veto in respect to acts of Parliament. New

[49] Thomas Jefferson, *A Summary View of the Rights of British America* (New York, 1943), p. 19.
[50] *Ibid.*, pp. 8 ff.   [51] *Ibid.*, pp. 7, 16, 22.

states produced new and sometimes opposing interests, and it was likely that these interests would become subjects of legislation which would exceed the legal limits of the legislatures enacting it.[52]

Jefferson complained of the king's bias in dealing with the various parts of the Empire. While the king had ceased to exercise his negative on the legislature of Great Britain, his vetoes of acts passed by the colonial legislatures were notorious. Though he no longer used his power of dissolving the British Parliament, he frequently dissolved the American legislatures. The king was called upon by Jefferson to cease sacrificing the rights of one part of the Empire "to the inordinate desires of another."[53]

As a document which was mainly from the pen of Jefferson, the Declaration of Independence of 1776 might be expected to reflect his views regarding the nature of the Empire. The principal emphasis of the Declaration is placed not upon the rights of the colonies as political communities but upon the rights of individuals. However, it is implicit in the Declaration that its authors understood the Empire to be an empire of many political communities which were on a level of equality with one another and connected only through the king. They did not recognize the Parliament of Great Britain as having any sovereign authority whatever over America. It was against the king that they directed the charge that colonial rights had been abused, and it was from the king that independence was declared. Parliament was mentioned by implication in the Declaration as a body which the king had unconstitutionally allowed to establish itself over America.

> He has combined with others to subject us to a jurisdiction foreign to our constitution, and unacknowledged by our laws; giving his Assent to their acts of pretended legislation: . . .
> For taking away our charters, abolishing our most valuable laws, and altering fundamentally the forms of our governments:

[52] *Ibid.*, p. 16.   [53] *Ibid.*, pp. 16, 18-19, 23.

For suspending our own legislatures, and declaring themselves invested with power to legislate for us in all cases whatsoever.[54]

Conclusion

The colonial arguments in support of the rights of the colonies indicate clearly that the idea of a political system comprised of constitutionally separate governments had taken strong hold in America by the end of the colonial era; and it is reasonable to surmise that the firm roots of this idea account in considerable degree for the later success of federalism in America. Yet one is not to assume that there was any general disposition among colonial leaders to regard the British Empire as falling within the category of federal systems. If there is any important evidence to the contrary, it is in an account in Jefferson's "Autobiography" relating to the debates in the Second Continental Congress on the proposal for a declaration of independence from the mother country. Jefferson notes in the "Autobiography" that "J. Adams, Lee, Wythe and others" referred to the connection between the colonies and the people and Parliament of England as a "federal connection."[55] But this autobiography, written late in the author's life and undoubtedly dependent largely on memory, could hardly be expected to represent with complete accuracy the terms used in 1776. If the term "federal" was actually used then to describe the relation of the colonies to England, the probability is that this usage was suggested because it was assumed that the colonies had given their tacit consent to have Parliament regulate their trade with the outside world. In any event, the term as used in the eighteenth century to refer to relations among political entities customarily carried with it the idea of contract. It was not broad enough to include any and all constitutional distributions of powers among such entities, although it is frequently used in this broad sense today.

[54] *Journals of the Continental Congress, 1774-1789*, ed. W. C. Ford (Washington, 1906), V, 512-13.
[55] Thomas Jefferson, *Writings*, library ed. (Washington, 1903-04), I, 21-22.

It was . . . thought that by the frequent meetings together of commissioners or representatives from all the colonies, the circumstances of the whole would be better known, and the good of the whole better provided for; and that the colonies would, by this connexion, learn to consider themselves, not as so many independent states, but as members of the same body; and thence be more ready to afford assistance and support to each other, and to make diversions in favor even of the most distant, and to join cordially in any expedition for the benefit of all against the common enemy.

—Benjamin Franklin commenting on the Albany plan of union. *The Complete Works of Benjamin Franklin,* ed. John Bigelow, II, 354.

(2)

Plans of Union

INSOFAR AS FEDERALISM IS CONCERNED, THE DEBATES of the colonial era over the nature of the British Empire surpass in importance all other American debates until 1787, when the Federal Constitutional Convention met. Any attempt to survey the history of American federalism, however, should include some attention to the New England Confederation, which existed from 1643 until 1684, when the Massachusetts Charter was revoked by royal decree; to the American Confederation of the period 1781-1789; and to some of the colonial plans of union which were proposed but never adopted. These unions and unadopted plans of union indicate some of the prevailing ideas about the institutional features of federal systems created when pre-existing political entities are brought together. Moreover, some idea of colonial notions on the location of sovereignty in federal systems is revealed in the discussions relating to the New England Confederation and the Albany plan of union of 1754. These will be considered later in this chapter.

The Institutional Features

The New England Confederation was based on articles of agreement among the general courts of Massachusetts, Connecticut, Plymouth, and New Haven, colonies which comprised the membership of the Confederation.[1] Its central au-

[1] A copy of the Articles is included in *Winthrop's Journal*, ed. J. K. Hosmer (New York, 1908), II, 100-05.

thority was a commission to which each of the general courts sent two representatives. This body was authorized to "hear, examine, weigh, and determine all affairs of war and peace," to admit new members into the Confederation, and to "frame and establish agreements and orders in general cases of a civil nature" touching intercolonial and external relations. The concurrence of six of the total of eight commissioners was sufficient to make a binding decision. When this majority was not obtained, the matter under consideration might be referred to the several general courts, and, in the event of such referral, a binding decision was arrived at by the concurrence of all of the general courts.

A plan submitted by William Penn to the British Board of Trade in 1697 called for the establishment of a central "congress," to which each of the colonies was to be entitled to send two deputies.[2] The primary function of this congress was to be that of settling disputes between colonies. But the powers of the congress were to be more extensive than those of the usual arbitral body. It was to be authorized to deal with questions relating to the disposition of criminals who fled from one colony to another, was to seek to "prevent or cure injuries in point of commerce," and was to provide for defense against "public enemies."

Daniel Coxe, a son of one of the proprietors of the Carolinas, proposed in 1726 the establishment of a "grand council" to be composed of deputies chosen by the colonies, each of the colonies being permitted to elect two deputies. It was to make provisions for the defense of the colonies, stipulating the quotas of men and money to be supplied by them for military purposes. A governor was to serve with the council, and this official and the council were to be vested with "jurisdictions,

[2] The documentary draft of Penn's plan may be found in the British *Calendar of State Papers,* Colonial Ser., America and West Indies, XV, 354-55, and in H. E. Egerton's *Federations and Unions within the British Empire* (Oxford, 1911), pp. 112-13.

powers and authorities, respecting the honour of His Majesty, the interest of the plantations, and the liberty and property of the proprietors, traders, planters and inhabitants."[3]

The Albany plan provided for a "grand council" and also called for an executive head, who was to have the title of "president-general."[4] The membership of the council was to be made up of persons elected by the colonial assemblies, the representation to be distributed among the colonies in proportion to their contributions to the general treasury but with the proviso that no colony would be allowed more than seven nor be restricted to less than two representatives. The council was to be authorized to declare war against the Indians. It was to provide for the "raising and paying of soldiers," the erection of forts, and the maintenance of a coast guard. The council and president-general were to be authorized to conclude treaties with the Indians, to regulate trade with them, and to purchase land from them for the British Crown. They were to be empowered to make grants to settlers of such lands as were purchased and were to make laws for governing settlements on these lands until the Crown should decide to organize the settlements "into particular governments." Although the general treasury was to be supplied in part by requisitions on the treasuries of the member colonies, the council and president-general were to be authorized to levy such "general duties, imposts, or taxes" as to them should appear most nearly equal and just in view of the ability and other circumstances of the inhabitants of the several colonies. They might select a general

[3] Coxe outlines his plan in his *A Description of the English Province of Carolina, by the Spaniards Called Florida, and by the French La Louisiana* (London, 1726), preface.
[4] A copy of the draft of the Albany plan appears in *Collections of the Massachusetts Historical Society for the Year 1800*, 1st Ser., VII, 203-07. For an early draft of the plan see Benjamin Franklin's "Short Hints toward a Scheme for Uniting the Northern Colonies," *The Complete Works of Benjamin Franklin*, ed. John Bigelow (New York, 1887-88), II, 345-47. Some comments on the "Short Hints" are in this same collection, II, 347 ff.

treasurer and, where necessary, might select treasurers to serve in the governments of the member colonies. On the other hand, the military and civil establishments of the colonies were to remain undisturbed. There was to be no impressment of men in any colony for military purposes without the consent of that colony's legislative assembly.

A plan of union proposed by Joseph Galloway in 1774 to the first Continental Congress and intended for eventual submission to the British king and Parliament called for a "president-general," to be appointed by the Crown, and for a "grand council," to be elected by the several colonial assemblies.[5] Representation in the council was to be distributed unequally among the colonies, although the specific basis for the apportionment of this representation was left for later determination. The jurisdiction of the president-general and council was to extend to matters relating to defense, general police affairs, and commercial matters. On the other hand, matters having to do with "internal police" were to be specifically reserved to the member colonies.

Quite evidently Galloway intended his plan to serve as a basis for a reconstruction of the British Empire insofar as relations between the colonies and the imperial government were concerned. Although the members of the council were to be elected locally, the council was to function as an "inferior and distinct branch" of the British Parliament, and measures initiated and adopted in the American branch were to be subject to veto by Parliament sitting in England. However, this right of veto was not to extend to defense measures adopted during emergencies, provided such measures received the approval of the president-general.

Galloway's plan was only one of numerous proposals for union put forward during the great controversy with England which ended in the independence of the American colonies. But few of these proposals did much more than emphasize the

[5] See *Journals of the Continental Congress, 1774-1789*, ed. W. C. Ford (Washington, 1904), I, 49-51.

desirability of a durable union.[6] The most important of them was the plan embodied in the Articles of Confederation framed in 1777 and finally brought into force in 1781 following ratification by the legislatures of the then thirteen states. Although the basic features of the government provided for in these Articles are generally known to students of American history, some of these features should be recalled here, particularly in view of the effect they had in molding the thinking of the 1780's on the institutions of federal government and in view of the great number of references to them during the framing and ratification of the United States Constitution.[7] The central authority provided for in the Articles was a Congress composed of representatives chosen in the states in such manner as the state legislatures directed. Representation and voting rights in this body were based strictly on the principle of state equality, each state being allowed to send as many as seven representatives but to cast through the representatives it sent only one vote on any measure before the body. There was no general rule, however, that actions taken by the Congress had first to receive the assent of all of the states. On relatively minor matters, a simple majority of the votes was all that was required, while on other matters action could be taken if it were supported by the votes of nine states. Broad powers in the fields of foreign affairs and defense, as well as other important powers, were delegated to the Congress. Specifically, the Congress could conclude treaties with foreign countries, declare war, regulate Indian affairs, borrow money, coin money and regulate its value, establish a postal system, and provide for the punishment of persons guilty of piracy or other felonies committed on the high seas.

The plans of union described in the foregoing paragraphs

[6] For some of these proposals see *American Archives*, 4th Ser., Vol. IV, cols. 467-68; Vol. V, cols. 450-52; Vol. VI, cols. 840-43.
[7] For an authentic text of the Articles of Confederation see the *Journals of the Continental Congress, 1774-1789*, ed. Gaillard Hunt (Washington, 1909), XIX, 214-23.

are to be included along with the colonial arguments over the
nature of the British Empire as evidence of the firm roots
which federalism had in early America. In addition, they
furnish a clue to the thinking of the colonial and Revolutionary periods regarding the general institutional pattern of federalism. The most important of the conclusions to which we
are led is that most of the planners thought in terms of the
league-type of union. That the member entities ought to be
treated as equals in every respect seems generally to have been
taken for granted, although it is true that the principle of
member equality was departed from in provisions for the composition of the councils in the Albany and Galloway plans.
Nor does it appear that the sponsors of the various plans of
union gave much thought to the possibility or desirability of
establishing direct relationships between the central organization and the inhabitants of the colonies or states, if indeed
they thought that such direct relationships would be in keeping with the principle of federalism. It is reasonable to assume
that the monetary exactions called for in the Albany plan
were intended to be imposed directly on inhabitants.[8] Also,
there was one provision of the Articles of 1781 which authorized the Confederation Congress to adopt coercive measures
directly applying to individual persons. This was the provision for dealing with piracy and other felonies committed on
the high seas—a provision that was to be relied on by strong
unionists in 1787 and 1788 to support their contention that
the inhabitants within a federal system might be brought
under the direct control of a central legislature without violating the federal principle. Nevertheless the fact remains that
the planners of union before 1787 usually thought in terms of
a division of authority that meant allotting to the central

[8] The Albany plan is interpreted as providing for direct relationships between the envisioned central establishment and individual persons in an
article by R. W. Kelsey, "The Originator of the Federal Idea," *The Nation*, XCIV (1912), 562-63, and in a committee report to the General
Assembly of Connecticut, *Collections . . . for the Year 1800*, 1st Ser.,
VII, 207-09.

establishment only the most general concerns. The legislative assemblies of the union members would pass the laws that might require for their enforcement the coercion of individual persons within the members' territorial limits.

The Problem of Sovereignty

It was noted in the preceding chapter that the federalist conceptions of the British Empire entertained by the American colonists had to compete with the notion of an illimitable sovereignty. One should therefore not be surprised to find that the idea of a federal union created by the bringing together of pre-existing political entities had to compete with this same notion. The notion was never so clearly expressed in connection with any of the plans of union as it was in connection with relations of the colonies to England, but in some of these plans a struggling with this notion is evident.

The ultimate sovereignty of the British Empire, when appealed to in answer to claims that the colonies possessed exclusive rights, was held to rest in Parliament. Parliament was assumed to be the source of all powers legitimately exercised by public bodies in America, and it was assumed to have the right to reclaim these powers. These assumptions, if agreed to, could but lead to the further assumption that Parliament must be the ultimate sovereign over any political unions created in America during the colonial period. Since some of the colonial plans of union were intended to be brought into force by Parliamentary enactment, it might be argued that their sponsors implicitly admitted the overriding sovereignty of Parliament. But this would not be true of the New England Confederation, which was formed by the member colonies without any reference to Parliament.[9] Nor would it be true

[9] The formation of the New England Confederation was in fact considered by some British authorities as evidence of the member colonies' disloyalty to England. Note, for example, the following communication of "His Majesty's Commissioners to Governor Prince," dated 1664:

We desire that when you send us your assent to the third proposition.

of the Confederation of 1781, whose basic Articles were drafted and ratified only after the colonies were declared to be independent states. In this Confederation the issue of sovereignty was dealt with by an express declaration in the Articles that each state in the union retained its sovereignty, although what is to be understood by the term sovereignty as used in the declaration is not clear.

The New England Confederation was entered into by the member colonies as "a firm and perpetual league of friendship and amity, for offense and defense, mutual advice and succor," and, as has already been mentioned, six of the eight commissioners who comprised the central establishment were given the right to bind the whole. The eleventh of the Articles of union provided that a breach of the Articles by one of the confederates was to be duly "ordered and considered" by the commissioners representing the other jurisdictions. But there was in this Confederation a controversy over the extent of the powers of the commissioners—the Massachusetts General Court, for instance, claimed something like absolute sovereignty. The controversy arose in 1652 when demands were made within the Confederation for military action against the Dutch settlements near the Delaware River.[10] Connecticut and New Haven both held that the Dutch were responsible for

---

you would let it, and the other three, be fairly written together, that they may be presented to His Majesty. And that, at the end of them, you would add something to this purpose, That the articles of confederation, when the four colonies entered into an offensive and defensive league, neither did, nor shall oblige you, to refuse His Majesty's authority, though any one, or all of the other three, should do so: not that we have the least imagination of your denying your obedience to His Majesty, but that we might stop some foul mouths in America, and that His Majesty may be the more confirmed in his good opinion of your loyalty, who has informed us (as we are told) that, that union was a war combination made by the four colonies, when they had a design to throw off their dependence on England, and for that purpose. *Collections of the Massachusetts Historical Society for the Year 1798,* 1st Ser., V, 192-93.

[10] For a short account of the controversy see C. M. Andrews, *Colonial Self-Government, 1652-1689* (New York, 1904), pp. 42-43.

certain Indian massacres, and Connecticut complained that the Dutch were interfering with her traders. The two colonies were able to get seven of the commissioners to agree that the "encroachments" of the Dutch called for a declaration of war, while the eighth commissioner, a representative of Massachusetts, dissented from the declaration and contested the right of the seven to bind the whole in a matter of this nature. His position was supported by the Massachusetts General Court, and, as a consequence, a general controversy ensued between the General Court and the majority of the commissioners.

This group relied on the expressed provisions of the Articles of union. Conceding that each colony had a right to its own "peculiar jurisdiction," they insisted that the commissioners had been granted the final "power of determining" with respect to the subjects committed to their charge and that no one colony could legally reject their decisions unless these decisions were "manifestly unjust."[11] On the other hand, the Massachusetts General Court took the position that supreme authority within the Confederation was in the several general courts of the members, insisting in effect that each of these general courts had the right to determine for itself what powers had been granted to the commissioners. Said the Massachusetts General Court in one of the statements it issued regarding the powers of the commissioners:

> It can be no less than a contradiction to affirm the supreme power (which we take to be the general courts in each jurisdiction) can be commanded by others; an absurdity in policy that an entire government and jurisdiction should prostitute itself to the command of strangers; a scandal to religion, that a general court of Christians should be obliged to act and engage upon the faith of six delegates, against their conscience—all which must be admitted in case, if we acknowledge ourselves bound to undertake an offensive war, upon the bare determination of the commis-

[11] *Records of the Governor and Company of the Massachusetts Bay,* ed. Nathaniel Shurtleff (Boston, 1853-54), IV, Pt. I, 168.

sioners, who cannot, nor ever did, challenge authority over us, or expect subjection from us. . . .

A fundamental law of a people or commonwealth is, to have liberty and to exercise immediate choice of their own governors, because the supreme governors are betrusted with their lives and estates, in whom, under God, they do acquiesce; but if they delegate others, in the aid of themselves, that are immediately chosen, then they may elect or accept of strangers, that is to say, such as are of another commonwealth; and such delegates may also, upon the same ground, impower others, and that without restriction of nation or number; which principle must needs be destructive to such a commonwealth, for then they may act to make an offensive war, which is an act of power in the highest nature.[12]

The Massachusetts General Court would not admit that the commissioners constituted a real governing authority. It explained that commissioners had been chosen by the general courts to be the general courts' counsel in these "weighty affairs," not to be their governors to command or enjoin them.[13] Since the "supreme powers of the several jurisdictions could not assemble," they had been forced to substitute delegates "to order such things as were of present or urgent necessity, or merely prudential and political, or of inferior nature." Matters, however, which required "the highest acts of authority," such as an "offensive war," were "in their nature of moral consideration." The "contrivers" of the confederacy had not seen fit to refer these matters of "highest concernment" to the commissioners.[14] Summing up its argument, the General Court declared:

. . . we cannot grant that the several jurisdictions are subordinate or subject to the authority of the commissioners, and therefore [the several jurisdictions are] not bound, in foro civili, to execute their determinations, nor act according to their judgments in making offensive war, leagues, or aides, because potestas belli

[12] This statement is from a committee report which was approved by the Massachusetts General Court. *Ibid.*, IV, Pt. I, 143.
[13] *Ibid.*, IV, Pt. I, 167.   [14] *Ibid.*, IV, Pt. I, 142.

gerendi aut pacis sanciendae, salva majestate imperii eripi nequit;
notwithstanding, if their judgment and determination be just and
according to the word of God, we do acknowledge the colonies
to be bound to act accordingly, not only in foro conscientiae, because the determinations are just, but in foro civili, because of the
contract and league between the confederates, although not by
the authority of the commissioners.[15]

The controversy between the Massachusetts General Court
and the majority group among the commissioners subsided
when the threat of war with the Dutch was removed.[16] However, the controversy affords an early American example of a
readiness among political entities, banded together under a
compact of union, to assume that they have an inherent sovereignty which includes a right to determine finally upon the
extent of their obligations when differences arise between
them and the union over the latter's jurisdictional sphere.
This assumption was not easily combated in the New England
Confederation, for, after all, this Confederation provided no
settled way of resolving such differences. Indeed, a settled
way of resolving such differences was not included in any of
the plans of union before the United States Constitution.

The drafters of the Albany plan of union were sensible of
difficulties that might arise over the problem of sovereignty
if precautions were not taken to avoid these difficulties. They
tacitly recognized the overriding sovereignty of Parliament,
for they decided that the union which they envisaged should
be established by an act of Parliament. However, they had
reasons for this decision which had nothing to do with the
question of imperial sovereignty. They surmised that it would
be difficult to get all of the colonies to enter voluntarily into

---

[15] *Ibid.*, IV, Pt. I, 168.
[16] The right to engage the Confederation in an offensive war was expressly denied to the commissioners in a revision of the Articles of Confederation in 1672 when the membership of the Confederation had been
reduced from four to three by the absorption of New Haven into Connecticut. See Article II of the revised Articles. *Ibid.*, IV, Pt. II, 477-83.

an agreement to establish a union, and that if such an agreement were actually entered into by the colonies, they might withdraw from it by repealing their several acts of ratification. Benjamin Franklin, one of the principal participants in the drafting convention at Albany, sets forth these reasons in an account of the deliberations of the convention.

> When it was considered that the colonies were seldom all in equal danger at the same time, or equally near the danger, or equally sensible of it, that some of them had particular interests to manage, with which a union might enterfere, and that they were extremely jealous of each other, it was thought impracticable to obtain a joint agreement of all the colonies to a union, in which the expense and burthen of defending any of them should be divided among them all; and if ever acts of assembly in all the colonies could be obtained for that purpose, yet as any colony, on the least dissatisfaction, might repeal its own act, and thereby withdraw itself from the union, it would not be a stable one, or such as could be depended on; for if only one colony should, on any disgust, withdraw itself, others might think it unjust and unequal that they, by continuing in the union, should be at the experise of defending a colony which refused to bear its proportional part, and would therefore one after another withdraw, till the whole crumbled into its original parts. Therefore the commissioners came to another previous resolution, *That it was necessary the union should be established by act of Parliament.*[17]

The important conclusion to be drawn from this statement by Franklin and from the position taken by the Massachusetts General Court on the proposed declaration of war against the Dutch is that the doctrine of contract in the seventeenth and eighteenth centuries was not conducive to the creation of a strong and durable union, if that union was to rest on no other foundation than an agreement among the colonies. It is true that Franklin gives no indication that the delegates assembled at Albany themselves subscribed to the notion that a colony

[17] Franklin, II, 352.

had a legal right to withdraw from a union which it had entered by solemn compact. But his statement constitutes clear evidence that these delegates assumed that there were some who would be likely to claim this right for a colony once they became dissatisfied with the union.

Hearken not to the voice which petulantly tells you that the form of government recommended for your adoption is a novelty in the political world; that it has never yet had a place in the theories of the wildest projectors; that it rashly attempts what it is impossible to accomplish. No, my countrymen, shut your ears against this unhallowed language. Shut your hearts against the poison which it conveys; the kindred blood which flows in the veins of American citizens, the mingled blood which they have shed in defense of their sacred rights, consecrate their union, and excite horror at the idea of their becoming aliens, rivals, enemies. . . . Is it not the glory of the people of America, that, whilst they have paid a decent regard to the opinions of former times and other nations, they have not suffered a blind veneration for antiquity, for custom, or for names, to overrule the suggestions of their own good sense, the knowledge of their own situation, and the lessons of their own experience? To this manly spirit, posterity will be indebted for the possession, and the world for the example, of the numerous innovations displayed on the American theater, in favor of private rights and public happiness.

—James Madison in the *Federalist*, ed. E. G. Bourne, I, No. 14, 93-94.

We have erred through excess of caution, and a zeal false and impracticable. Our counsels have been destitute of consistency and stability. I am flattered with the hope . . . that we have now found a cure for the evils under which we have so long labored. I trust that the proposed constitution affords a genuine specimen of representative and republican government; and that it will answer, in an eminent degree, all the beneficial purposes of society.

—Alexander Hamilton addressing the convention called in New York to ratify the United States Constitution. *Debates in the Several State Conventions on the Adoption of the Federal Constitution*, ed. Jonathan Elliot, 2nd edition (1836), II, 254.

(3)

Creating the "More Perfect" Union

THE FIRST OCCASION IN AMERICAN HISTORY IN WHICH both theoretical and practical aspects of federalism were extensively discussed occurred during the debates over the framing and ratification of the United States Constitution. These debates ranged over almost every conceivable aspect of the institutional arrangements of federal systems, and touched upon many, if indeed not most, of the important legal questions relating to federalism which were later to engage the attention of American constitutional theorists. The great issue in the debates was, of course, whether the union under the Articles of Confederation of 1781 was to be abandoned in favor of a much stronger union, the establishment of which would necessarily mean a drastic curtailment of state powers. It will be helpful in connection with what follows to have in mind several of the features of the new union which were intended to give it strength. First, it was to be based, not on a compact or treaty ratified by the state legislatures but on a document which, in theory at least, was to be assented to by those qualified to vote in the states. Second, while the method of choosing the members of the Congress under the Articles of 1781 was left to be determined by the state legislatures, popular election was to be the one and only method of choosing the members of one of the houses of the new central legislature. Third, while the states had equal voting rights in the existing Congress, in the composition of the new government the principle of state equality was to be blended with the principle of allotting representation among the states on the basis of their populations. Fourth, the new Congress was, with respect to many subjects, to be allowed to pass laws which would apply to individual persons and which would be enforced through a federal executive and a system of federal courts.

Some of these features were embodied in the Virginia plan of union introduced early in the proceedings of the Federal Convention of 1787, and although this plan was departed from in certain important particulars, these several features were embodied in the Constitution as finally drafted and adopted. Quite understandably some of them were subjects of extended debate as the Constitution went through the process of being drafted and ratified.

The Arguments for the New Union

The side of the supporters of the new union was greatly strengthened by having in Hamilton and Madison two men who were keenly aware of the weaknesses which had been characteristic of most previously formed federal systems and who possessed the skill requisite for pointing out these weaknesses. They gave detailed attention to them in the *Federalist* essays which they authored to win support for ratification of the Constitution in New York State. In addition, certain of the weaknesses were stressed by them as delegates in the Federal Convention and as delegates in the New York and Virginia ratifying conventions, respectively.

In discussing the weaknesses of federal systems, Hamilton and Madison were obviously thinking principally of political unions which had been formed by compact among pre-existing governments and in which the governments continued to stand as intermediaries between the central establishments created and the individual citizens. Both men clearly wished the new American union to be founded on a basis that would be as solid as the British constitution in the colonial era, although there is little evidence to indicate that either of them thought of the British Empire as affording a federal precedent for the proposed new union. Both regarded a compact among governments to create a federal system as falling in the general category of ordinary treaties among nations and considered it already demonstrated that the parties to such instruments were not to be depended upon to observe them in good faith. Madison's thinking on this matter is well illustrated in a statement he made before the Federal Convention expressing the hope that the document that was to emerge from the Convention would not have the character of a treaty among nations. He remarked that he considered the difference between a system founded on the legislatures and one founded on the people to be the true difference between a league or treaty and a constitution. He explained:

. . . The former in point of *moral obligation* might be as inviolable as the latter. In point of *political operation*, there were two important distinctions in favor of the latter. 1. A law violating a treaty ratified by a pre-existing law, might be respected by the judges as a law, though an unwise or perfidious one. A law violating a constitution established by the people themselves, would be considered by the judges as null and void. 2. The doctrine laid down by the law of nations in the case of treaties is that a breach of any one article by any of the parties, frees the other parties from their engagements. In the case of a union of people under one constitution, the nature of the pact has always been understood to exclude such an interpretation. Comparing the two modes [of ratifying the United States Constitution] in point of expediency . . . all the considerations which recommended this Convention in preference to Congress for proposing the reform were in favor of state conventions in preference to the legislatures for examining and adopting it.[1]

In the *Federalist* Hamilton argued for the abandonment in America of the idea of a union based on a compact among the states. "The fabric of American empire ought to rest on

[1] *Records of the Federal Convention of 1787*, ed. Max Farrand (New Haven, 1911), II, 93. For other statements by Madison of his views on the effect of ratification by the state legislatures see I, 122-23, 126-27.

the solid basis of the consent of the people."² The fact that the
existing Articles of Confederation had never had a ratification
by the people had contributed in no small way to the infirmi-
ties of the union for which they provided. Resting on no
better foundation than the consent of the state legislatures, the
union had been exposed to frequent and intricate questions
concerning the "validity" of its powers, and there had even
arisen in some instances the "enormous" doctrine that a state
had a right to repeal the act by which its approval of the
Articles had been given.³ The effect of having the Constitution ratified by popularly elected state conventions rather
than by state legislatures was not elaborated upon by Hamilton, but he seems clearly to have assumed that ratification by
the state conventions would render it unlikely that the Constitution would later be regarded as a compact among states.

But, in Hamilton's view, to abandon the idea of a union
based on a compact among states was no more important
than to abandon the idea that the central establishment created
should deal almost exclusively with corporate entities. In other
words, it was of the utmost importance that the central establishment be given broad powers to deal directly with individual
persons, as provided in the new Constitution. The bane of the
existing Confederation, Hamilton contended, had been the
predominance of the principle of legislating for states or governments. He explained that this principle ultimately determined how far the Confederation Congress could go in
achieving the purposes of union, observing that the Congress
could obtain troops and revenues only through requisitions
upon the states—requisitions which were in practice mere
recommendations which the states honored or disregarded at
their option.⁴

The principle of legislating for states was defective for two
reasons: First, individual persons, when acting singly, more

---

² The *Federalist*, ed. E. G. Bourne (Washington and London, 1901), I, No.
22, 151.
³ *Ibid.*, I, No. 22, 150.   ⁴ *Ibid.*, I, No. 15, 99-100.

readily acted with rectitude (i.e., in obedience to law) than they did when acting in organized groups, including states. Second, the love of power of those intrusted with the affairs of a state would cause them to look with an evil eye on attempts to restrain or direct the state's operations. When laws were directed at individual persons, obedience to them was secured by the mild coercion of the magistracy, but when they were directed at states, the securing of obedience must frequently require resort to military force.[5]

The weakness of federal systems is the subject of Numbers 18 through 20 of the *Federalist,* commonly attributed to Hamilton and Madison as joint authors although the evidence definitely points to Madison as the one who supplied nearly all of the material and who actually wrote the three papers.[6] Fairly detailed attention is given in these papers to the Amphictyonic and Achaean confederacies among the ancient Greeks and to the German (Holy Roman Empire), Swiss, and Netherlands confederacies. The histories of all of these systems are found to have been marked by internal dissensions, foreign intrigue, and warfare. Even the Achaean confederacy, whose organization is adjudged to have been superior, is found to have suffered frequent and serious disruptions, until it finally came to its end. Macedon had practiced the arts of division among its member cities, and, as a result, the union had been dissolved. It had been re-formed only to fall later under the mastery first of Macedon and then of Rome. The Romans had fostered dissensions among the cities and had finally seduced them from the League "by representing to their pride the violation it committed on their sovereignty."[7] The general discussion of the vicissitudes of the several systems closes with a warning which emphasizes that great care

[5] *Ibid.,* I, No. 15, 101 ff.
[6] See the article by Douglass Adair on "The Authorship of the Disputed Federalist Papers," *William and Mary Quarterly,* 3rd Ser., I (1944), 97–122, 235–64, especially pp. 104–05, 116–17, 249–50.
[7] The *Federalist,* I, No. 18, 122.

is required in the construction of a federal organization to insure the presence of sufficient energy at the common center.

I make no apology for having dwelt so long on the contemplation of these federal precedents. Experience is the oracle of truth; and where its responses are unequivocal, they ought to be conclusive and sacred. The important truth, which it unequivocally pronounces in the present case, is that a sovereignty over sovereigns, a government over governments, a legislation for communities, as contradistinguished from individuals, as it is a solecism in theory, so in practice it is subversive of the order and ends of civil polity, by substituting *violence* in place of *law*, or the destructive *coercion* of the *sword* in place of the mild and salutary *coercion* of the *magistracy*.[8]

Generally opponents of the proposed Constitution argued that the powers contemplated for the central government would endanger the continued existence of the states. But convinced as they were of a tendency inherent in federal systems for the "subordinate or inferior orbs" to fly off from the common center, Hamilton and Madison professed to believe that it was highly improbable that the new government would ever encroach upon the reserved jurisdictions of the states. To satisfy the opponents, however, they called attention to the roles which the states were to have in the composition of the new government and to local influences which might be expected to favor the states in any contest for power between the new government and the state governments.[9] The importance which they placed on these influences is illustrated by Hamilton's comments upon them in the *Federalist*.

It is a known fact in human nature, that its affections are commonly weak in proportion to the distance or diffusiveness of the object. Upon the same principle that a man is more attached to his

[8] *Ibid.*, I, No. 20, 134.
[9] For Hamilton's views on how the states would fare in the proposed new union see the *Federalist*, No. 17. For Madison's views on the same subject see *Ibid.*, Nos. 45 and 46.

family than to his neighborhood, to his neighborhood than to the
community at large, the people of each state would be apt to feel
a stronger bias towards their local governments than towards the
government of the union; unless the force of that principle should
be destroyed by a much better administration of the latter.

This strong propensity of the human heart would find powerful auxiliaries in the objects of state regulation.

This variety of more minute interests, which will necessarily
fall under the superintendence of the local administrations, and
which will form so many rivulets of influence, running through
every part of the society, cannot be particularized, without involving a detail too tedious and uninteresting to compensate for
the instruction it might afford.[10]

Hamilton went on to argue that the subjects to be dealt
with by the new central government were not of such a
character as to cause the people to have for this government
the same sense of attachment that they were to be expected to
have for their state governments if these administered their
affairs with uprightness and prudence. Confined to more general interests, the operations of the "national government"
would be less likely than those of the state governments "to
come home to the feelings of the people."[11]

The Requirements of Federalism

Most of the legal arguments relating to the proposed new
union tended to concentrate on the mandate to the Federal
Convention of 1787 to propose a revision of the existing
Articles of Confederation. No one questioned the authority
of the Convention to propose far-reaching changes, but the
question raised was whether the Convention had been authorized to proceed on any such basis as that suggested by the
Virginia plan or by the Constitution as finally drafted. Immediately following introduction of the Virginia plan in the
early proceedings of the Convention, it was labeled by pro-

[10] *Ibid.*, I, No. 17, 112-13.   [11] *Ibid.*, I, No. 17, 113.

ponents and opponents alike as a "national" plan, members of both groups clearly assuming that a national government and a federal government fell into two quite distinct categories.[12] Indeed, Edmund Randolph, chairman of the Virginia delegation in the Convention, offered, at the suggestion of Gouverneur Morris, resolutions in which it was declared that "a union of the states merely federal will not accomplish the objects proposed by the Articles of Confederation" and that "a *national* government ought to be established consisting of a *supreme* legislative [sic], executive & judiciary."[13]

At the beginning of the debates in the Convention, supporters of the Virginia plan as well as those opposing it assumed that a federal government was properly to be defined as a government erected by means of a compact among preexisting political entities. This seems clear from the resolutions offered by Randolph, in which the inadequacy of a treaty or treaties among the states as individual sovereignties is given as a reason for the declaration in favor of a national instead of a federal government. Gouverneur Morris went on to explain during the debate on the resolutions that a federal government was "a mere compact resting on the good faith of the parties," and that "a *national, supreme* government" had "a complete and *compulsive* operation."[14]

The supporters of the Virginia plan clearly assumed that the Convention was to be regarded as having a free hand to propose any changes from the existing Articles that it thought wise. On the other hand, those opposing the plan advanced the argument that the Convention was legally authorized to consider only federal proposals. Thus William Paterson of New

[12] For an analysis of the Virginia plan and an account of the proceedings of the Federal Convention thereon, see Max Farrand's *The Framing of the Constitution of the United States* (New Haven, 1913), Chap. V.
[13] Farrand, *Records*, I, 33.
[14] *Ibid.*, I, 34. Generally the references to the *Records* of the Federal Convention in this chapter are to Madison's notes on the proceedings of the Convention, although other notes on these proceedings are occasionally cited.

Jersey declared that the delegates in the Convention were assembled "as deputies of 13 independent, sovereign states, for federal purposes," that "the idea of a national government as contradistinguished from a federal one" had not entered into the minds of the states when the delegates had been commissioned to come to the Convention.[15] Generally Paterson and those siding with him assumed that a federal system must conform to the basic plan of organization of the existing American Confederation, regardless of which powers were allowed to the central establishment or how they were to be exercised. It is not clear whether they always intended to argue that the central establishment must be invested with no power to adopt laws directly applying to individual persons, although this argument was advanced by Luther Martin of Maryland and was assumed by Hamilton and Madison to be one of the principal arguments to be countered. The most common arguments advanced in opposition to the Virginia plan and to the Constitution as finally drafted were that a federal government was based on a compact among states, that members of the central legislative organ represented states, and that the states were equally represented in this organ. When independent societies confederated for mutual defense, said Paterson, they did so "in their collective capacity." Each state was to be considered "as *one* of the contracting parties."[16] Moreover, representation in the central legislature was apportioned equally among the states. Paterson declared: "A confederacy supposes sovereignty in the members composing it and sovereignty supposes equality."[17] This notion of a federal system was the basis of the New Jersey plan of union introduced by Paterson in the Federal Convention as a federal counterproposal to the Virginia plan. The union envisioned in the New Jersey plan was to be based upon articles of agreement among states, and states were to be equally represented in

[15] *Ibid.*, I, 178, 182.
[16] *Ibid.*, I, 250, 259.
[17] *Ibid.*, I, 178.

the central legislature, as they were in the existing Articles.[18]

Robert Lansing of New York considered the New Jersey plan to be federal because the central powers for which it provided were to flow "from the respective state governments." He professed to support this plan because he was of the opinion "that the power of the Convention was restrained to amendments of a federal nature, and having for their basis the Confederacy in being." A general government deriving its powers from the people of the states, he argued, must ultimately result in the destruction of the state governments.[19] Oliver Ellsworth and Gunning Bedford, delegates from Connecticut and Delaware, respectively, both supported the argument that equality of voting rights among member states was an essential aspect of a confederacy. Ellsworth asserted that there had been no example of a confederacy in which the members did not have an equality of voices.[20] Bedford asserted that the American states "must continue if not perfectly, yet equally sovereign" if a confederate system were decided upon by the Convention. Ostensibly with the equality principle in mind, he declared that there was "no middle way between a perfect consolidation and a mere confederacy of the states."[21]

Luther Martin, one of the most earnest supporters of the New Jersey plan and definitely the most vociferous one, defended it and opposed the Virginia plan and the Constitution as finally drafted by drawing upon the doctrine of the social contract. He argued that states when not united in a confederacy might be considered as in a state of nature with respect to each other, just as individuals were to be so considered before they contracted to enter civil society. Citing Locke, Vattel, and Rutherford as authorities, he insisted that states,

---

[18] For an analysis of the New Jersey plan and an account of the Convention proceedings thereon, see Farrand's *The Framing of the Constitution*, Chap. VI.

[19] Farrand, *Records*, I, 249, 257.

[20] *Ibid.*, I, 484.   [21] *Ibid.*, I, 490-91.

like individuals in a state of nature, were equally free until they surrendered "equal sovereignty." The separation of the American colonies from Great Britain had placed them in a state of nature with respect to each other, and but for the existing Confederation they would still be in this condition. They had entered into the Confederation on an equal footing, and they were now met to amend the Articles of Confederation on the same footing. They could not "treat or confederate so as to give up an equality of votes without giving up their liberty." Moreover, a federal government, being a government to preserve states, was a government to be instituted by the assent of states and not by the assent of their people. Legally the people of the United States could neither speak nor hear except through the state legislatures. A resort to the people for the creation of a new government would mean throwing them back into a state of nature and would consequently involve a dissolution of the existing state governments.[22]

Most of the delegates in the Federal Convention who opposed the Virginia plan on federal grounds appear to have been satisfied when the Convention reached its decision to propose a central legislature of two houses, one to be composed of representatives apportioned among the states on the basis of the distribution of population and one to be equally representative of all the states. Thus Ellsworth, one of the originators of this compromise, regarded it as a solution which could be expected to protect both the large states against the small and the small states against the large. He observed following the compromise that we were now "partly national; partly federal," explaining that the proportional representation feature of the first branch of the legislature was comfortable to the national principle and that the equality of voices contemplated for the second branch accorded with the federal principle.[23]

However, the controversy over the authority of the Federal

[22] *Ibid.*, I, 324, 329, 437-38.
[23] *Ibid.*, I, 468.

Convention and the nature of federal systems raged after the Convention adjourned. Martin bitterly criticized the work of the Convention in a report to the Maryland legislature in which he discussed in detail arguments that had been made in the Convention. He explained that the delegates in the Convention had been divided into two parties, attributing to one of these parties views which he himself had advanced. After elaborating upon ideas on the social contract which he associated with the "truly federal party," he continued:

> Having thus established these principles, with respect to the *rights of individuals* in a *state of nature*, and what is due to *each*, on entering into government, (principles established by every writer on liberty), they proceeded to show, that *states*, when *once formed*, are considered, *with respect* to *each other*, as *individuals* in a state of nature; that, like individuals, each *state* is considered *equally free* and *equally independent*, the one having no right to exercise authority *over* the other, though more *strong*, *more wealthy*, or *abounding with more inhabitants*. That, when a number of *states* unite themselves under *a federal government*, the *same principles apply to them, as when a number of individual men* unite themselves under a *state government*. That every argument which shows *one man* ought not to have *more votes* than *another*, because he is *wiser, stronger*, or *wealthier*, proves that *one state* ought not to have *more votes* than *another*, because it is *stronger, richer*, or *more populous*. And, that by *giving one state*, or *one or two states, more votes* than the *others*, the *others* thereby are *enslaved to such state or states*, having the *greater number of votes*, in the *same manner* as in the case before put, of *individuals*, when one has *more votes than the others*. That the reason why each individual man in forming a state government should have an equal vote, is because each individual, before he enters into government, is *equally free and independent*. So *each state*, when *states enter* into a federal government, are [sic] entitled to an equal vote; because, before they entered into such federal government, *each state was equally free* and *equally independent*. That *adequate* representation of *men formed into a state government*, consists in *each man* having an *equal voice*, either personally, or, if by representatives, that he should have an equal

voice in choosing the representatives. So, adequate representation of *states* in a *federal government*, consists in *each state* having an *equal voice*, either in person or by its representative, in every thing which relates to the federal government.[24]

Other opponents of the Constitution took the position that basing the document on the people rather than on the state governments would necessarily mean a departure from federal principles. Samuel Nason, a delegate in the Massachusetts Ratifying Convention, professed to believe that the phrase "we the people of the United States" in the preamble to the proposed Constitution implied an "annihilation of the state governments." He reasoned, though somewhat vaguely, that a vote for adoption of the Constitution would be a vote to abandon a federal system properly created and to bring about "a perfect consolidation of the whole union."

When . . . we dissolved the political bands which connected us with Great Britain, we were in a state of nature. We then formed and adopted the Confederation, which must be considered as a sacred instrument; this confederates us under one head, as sovereign and independent states. Now . . . if we give Congress power to dissolve that Confederation, to what can we trust? If a nation consent thus to treat their most solemn compacts, who will ever trust them? . . . We are under oath: we have sworn that Massachusetts is a sovereign and independent state. How then can we vote for this constitution, that destroys that sovereignty?[25]

Similar views were expressed by Patrick Henry in the Virginia Ratifying Convention. He assumed it to be demonstrably clear that the proposed new government was to be a "consolidated government" and questioned the authority of the delegates in the Federal Convention to propose a document that was to be viewed as emanating from the people rather than from the states.

[24] *Ibid.*, III, 183.
[25] *Debates in the Several State Conventions on the Adoption of the Federal Constitution*, ed. Jonathan Elliot, 2nd ed. (Washington, 1836), II, 144.

I have the highest veneration for those gentlemen; but, sir, give me leave to demand, what right had they to say, *we the people?* My political curiosity, exclusive of my anxious solicitude for the public welfare, leads me to ask, who authorized them to speak the language of, *we the people,* instead of, *we the states?* States are the characteristics, and the soul of a confederation. If the states be not the agents of this compact, it must be one great consolidated national government, of the people of all the states.[26]

Henry argued that the people had no right to enter into leagues, alliances, or confederations. "States and foreign powers," he insisted, were the only proper agents for such purposes.[27]

Hamilton and Madison assumed the major responsibility for combating the notion of a federal system held by the opponents of the Virginia plan and of the Constitution as finally drafted, although these two men had strong support from James Wilson. Like Martin, Hamilton and Wilson both referred to the doctrine of the social contract as affording a clue to principles to be followed in the construction of federal systems, although they both meant for the doctrine to support views diametrically opposed to those of Martin. Hamilton observed in the Federal Convention that it was as reasonable for states to enter into a "league" departing from the principle of state equality as it was for men to enter into a "social compact" and to agree to depart from their natural equality.[28] Obviously intending to support the union proposed by the Federal Convention as a federal system, Wilson drew an analogy in the Pennsylvania Ratifying Convention between the position of states that had been united to create such a system and the position of individual persons who had been united under a state government.

In considering and developing the nature and end of the system before us, it is necessary to mention another kind of liberty, which has not yet, as far as I know, received a name. I shall dis-

[26] *Ibid.,* III, 54.   [27] *Ibid.,* III, 79.
[28] Farrand, *Records,* I, 477.

tinguish it by the appellation of *federal liberty*. When a single government is instituted, the individuals of which it is composed, surrender to it a part of their natural independence, which they before enjoyed as men. When a confederate republic is instituted, the communities, of which it is composed, surrender to it a part of their political independence, which they before enjoyed as states. The principles, which directed, in the former case, what part of the natural liberty of the man ought to be given up, and what part ought to be retained will give similar directions in the latter case. The states should resign to the national government, that part, and that part, only, of their political liberty, which, placed in that government, will produce more good to the whole, than if it had remained in the several states. While they resign this part of their political liberty, they retain the free and generous exercise of all their other faculties, as states, so far as it is compatible with the welfare of the general and superintending confederacy.[29]

However, it was mainly on precedents which they held to be afforded by earlier federalized systems and on the authority of Baron de Montesquieu that Hamilton, Madison, and Wilson relied as they sought to counter the opposition arguments. Contrary to what might be supposed, they appear never to have found any of the plans of union of colonial America of any usefulness as federal models; but they did refer for supporting precedents to several federalized systems that had been in existence. The power vested in the Congress of the existing American Confederation to enact laws for the punishment of piracy was referred to by both Hamilton and Madison as a precedent for permitting the new Congress to enact laws to be applied directly to individuals.[30] Madison went on to point out that the practice of Connecticut and Rhode Island was to choose by popular vote their representatives in the Confederation Congress—a practice which he regarded as a precedent for permitting the people to choose representatives

[29] Elliot, II, 403.   [30] Farrand, *Records*, I, 283, 314.

in the new Congress.[31] Hamilton found in the British Empire
of the colonial era a precedent for departing from the principle of state equality in the composition of the new Congress.
He explained that many parts of the Empire had had no representation whatever in Parliament and that notwithstanding this
fact Parliament had asserted a supremacy over the whole of
the Empire. This supremacy, he observed, had been accepted,
except for American objections in behalf of colonial rights.[32]
Hamilton also referred to the Holy Roman Empire as a "confederacy" which exhibited supporting precedents for the proposed new union. For example, he interpreted the fundamental
law of this Empire as permitting the Diet to legislate for individual persons.[33]

Although ancient leagues and confederacies were most
commonly referred to in the debates over the Constitution to
emphasize the weaknesses of federal systems, it was assumed
by Hamilton and Madison that the institutional arrangements
of the Achaean and Lycian confederacies supported a much
broader definition of federalism than that advanced by the
opponents of the Constitution.[34] The former of these two
confederacies was Greek, and while the latter existed outside
of Greece, it was in close proximity to Greece and was most
probably influenced by Greek institutions and practices. The
information available to the Americans of 1787 and 1788 which
related to the institutional arrangements of these two confederacies appears to have been quite limited, being drawn almost entirely from the Greek geographer Strabo, the Abbé
Mably, and Montesquieu. Madison himself was deeply conscious of a lack of information on the Achaean confederacy,

---

[31] Ibid., I, 314.   [32] Ibid., I, 472.
[33] Ibid., I, 283, 294.
[34] The institutional arrangements and history of the Achaean and Lycian
confederacies and also sources of information about them which were
available to the framers of the United States Constitution are discussed
by Edward A. Freeman in his History of Federal Government from the
Foundation of the Achaian League to the Disruption of the United States
(London, 1863), I, 208-17 and Chap. V, passim.

expressing regret that the monuments that remained of "this curious political fabric" were so imperfect.[35] In the Pennsylvania Ratifying Convention, James Wilson referred to the paucity of information about the Achaean, Lycian, and Amphictyonic confederacies. He stated that he had searched all of the books to which he had access for information about the "Lycian Republic" and reported that its history could not be found, that the few facts that related to it were mentioned only by Strabo. However excellent a model it might have been, the Federal Convention had been forced to work without it.[36] Even so, Hamilton and Madison professed to see striking analogies between the Achaean and Lycian confederacies and the plan of union proposed by the Federal Convention. They, and Charles Pinckney, all referred to the Lycian confederacy as affording a precedent for departing from the principle of state equality in determining the distribution of representation in the new Congress. They pointed out that votes in the common council of this confederacy had been distributed among the member cities in proportion to their size or, in the words of Madison, "their importance."[37] Hamilton observed that the vestiges that remained of the Achaean and Lycian confederacies indicated that these unions had been, of all the confederacies of antiquity, most nearly free of the "mistaken principle" of legislating for communities in their political capacities.[38] He also stated that the council of the Lycian confederacy had been invested with the authority to appoint all of the judges and magistrates of the member cities, though it is probable that his information on this matter was inaccurate.[39] Inso-

---

[35] The *Federalist*, I, No. 18, 119. It is taken for granted that the number of the *Federalist* here cited was written by Madison.

[36] Elliot, II, 397, 449.

[37] For a reference by Madison to the allotment of votes in the Lycian confederacy, see Farrand, *Records*, I, 485; for one by Hamilton, see the *Federalist*, I, No. 9, 61; for one by Pinckney, see *The Delegate from New York*, ed. J. R. Strayer (Princeton, 1939), p. 57.

[38] The *Federalist*, I, No. 16, 105.

[39] *Ibid.*, I, No. 9, 61, and Freeman, I, 209 and note.

far as precedents were concerned, Madison appears to have been most impressed by the principle of unequal voting of the Lycian confederacy. In any event, he surmised that the constitution of this confederacy was more like the plan of government proposed by the Federal Convention than that of any of the Greek leagues or confederacies.[40] However, he was also impressed by the intimacy of the Achaean union, concluding from the authorities he had consulted that the cities comprising this union had all had the same laws and customs, the same weights and measures, and the same currency. He noted that the role played by the central authority in bringing about this uniformity had been left in uncertainty, but thought it probable that the central authority had borne a considerable likeness, in both "degree and species of power," to the government to be established by the adoption of the new Constitution.[41]

In a chapter on "confederate republics" in his *Spirit of the Laws*, Montesquieu had represented this species of political organization as an expedient for avoiding despotism in a country of large geographical area, and had gone on to emphasize its possibilities for defensive purposes.[42] But it was in his definition of a confederate republic that the advocates of the proposed new union found some of their principal support. He had defined a confederate republic as a kind of assemblage of societies that constituted a new society.[43] This definition was certainly broad enough to embrace the proposed new union, a fact which undoubtedly commended it to Hamilton and to others. Indeed, Montesquieu praised the Lycian confederacy as "a model of an excellent confederate republic" and mentioned specifically that the members of this confederacy had been allotted votes in the common council on a proportional

[40] The *Federalist*, I, No. 45, 316.
[41] *Ibid.*, I, No. 18, 119; I, No. 45, 316.
[42] Montesquieu, *The Spirit of the Laws*, trans. Thomas Nugent (New York, 1949), pp. 126-27.
[43] *Ibid.*, p. 126.

basis and that this council had had the authority to appoint local magistrates.[44]

Hamilton and Wilson both referred to Montesquieu's definition of a confederate republic, Hamilton quite evidently regarding the adjective "confederate" as synonymous with the adjective "federal."[45] In the Pennsylvania Ratifying Convention Wilson, while not giving any indication that he considered the two adjectives synonymous, unhesitatingly referred to a confederate republic as defined by Montesquieu as having furnished the basic plan of governmental organization on which the Federal Convention had worked while it drew up the United States Constitution. Actually he thought of a confederate republic as falling between a loose union of states and a completely consolidated union, observing that there had been several associations of states which had been called "confederate states" but which had not in propriety of language deserved to be so labeled. He explained that the United Netherlands did not correspond with the full definition of a "confederate republic," noting that "this assemblage of societies" did not constitute a new society.[46]

Hamilton, Madison, and Wilson all referred to Montesquieu's selection of the Lycian confederacy as a model of excellence among confederate republics.[47] With specific reference to Montesquieu and his comments regarding the Lycian confederacy, Hamilton remarked: "Thus we perceive that the distinctions insisted upon [by the opponents of the proposed new union] were not within the contemplation of this enlightened civilian; and we shall be led to conclude, that they are the novel refinements of an erroneous theory."[48]

[44] *Ibid.*, p. 128.
[45] For references by Hamilton to this definition see Farrand, *Records,* I, 283, and the *Federalist,* I, No. 9, 59 ff. For a reference by Wilson to this definition see Elliot, II, 397.
[46] Elliot, II, 397.
[47] See Farrand, *Records,* I, 485; the *Federalist,* I, No. 9, 61; and Elliot, II, 449.
[48] The *Federalist,* I, No. 9, 61.

On the basis of the precedents to which he referred and on the authority of Montesquieu, Hamilton in effect concluded that there was no rule whatever which dictated the arrangements within a federal system aside from the rule that there must be a constitutional distribution of powers between the central establishment and the members of the system. He wrote:

> The extent, modifications, and objects of the federal authority are mere matters of discretion. So long as the separate organization of the members be not abolished; so long as it exists, by a constitutional necessity, for local purposes; though it should be in perfect subordination to the general authority of the union, it would still be, in fact and in theory, an association of states, or a confederacy. The proposed Constitution, so far from implying an abolition of the state governments, makes them constituent parts of the national sovereignty, by allowing them a direct representation in the Senate, and leaves in their possession certain exclusive and very important portions of sovereign power. This fully corresponds, in every rational import of the terms, with the idea of a federal government.[49]

Generally Madison was inclined toward acceptance of the broad definition of a federal system which was supported by Hamilton. Apparently, however, he recognized the difficulty of winning general acceptance of this definition. In any event, he finally chose to demonstrate to the opponents of the proposed new union that even on the basis of the most common understanding of the terms "federal" and "national," the government which was intended to be established would possess as many federal as national attributes. His demonstration was undertaken in the *Federalist* and in the Virginia Ratifying Convention by a careful analysis of pertinent provisions of the Constitution as it had come from the Federal Convention.[50]

Madison began by explaining that the real character of the proposed new government could be ascertained from the

[49] *Idem.*
[50] See the *Federalist*, No. 39; and Elliot, III, 114-15.

foundation on which it was to be established, from the sources from which its "ordinary powers" were to be drawn, from the operation and extent of those powers, and from the authority by which future changes were to be introduced. He held that the foundation of the government was to be federal on the ground that states were to be the parties to the Constitution. Although the Constitution was to be ratified by the people of America through elected deputies, the people were not to ratify "as individuals composing one entire nation" but "as composing the distinct and independent states" to which they belonged. The Constitution was to be put into effect neither by a majority of the people of the union nor by a majority of the states, but by the unanimous decision of the several states that became parties to it. The assent which the states were to give would differ from "their ordinary assent" only in that it would be given by the people in the states rather than by the state legislatures.[51]

When the new government was considered from the standpoint of the sources of its "ordinary powers," it was partly federal and partly national. The House of Representatives, de-

---

[51] "That it will be a federal and not a national act, as these terms are understood by the objectors; the act of the people, as forming so many independent states, not as forming one aggregate nation, is obvious from this single consideration, that it is to result neither from the decision of a *majority* of the people of the union, nor from that of a *majority* of the states. It must result from the *unanimous* assent of the several states that are parties to it, differing no otherwise from their ordinary assent than in its being expressed, not by the legislative authority, but by that of the people themselves. Were the people regarded in this transaction as forming one nation, the will of the majority of the whole people of the United States would bind the minority, in the same manner as the majority in each state must bind the minority; and the will of the majority must be determined either by a comparison of the individual votes, or by considering the will of the majority of the states as evidence of the will of a majority of the people of the United States. Neither of these rules have [sic] been adopted. Each state, in ratifying the Constitution, is considered as a sovereign body, independent of all others, and only to be bound by its own voluntary act. In this relation, then, the new Constitution will, if established, be a *federal*, and not a *national* Constitution." The *Federalist*, I, No. 39, 260.

riving its powers "from the people of America"—the people being "represented in the same proportion and on the same principle" as they were "in the legislature of a particular State"—would give the system a national aspect. On the other hand, the Senate, deriving its powers from the states "as political and coequal societies"—these societies being represented on a basis of equality—would give the system a federal character. Finally, the presidency in the derivation of its powers was to be both federal and national. The immediate election of the president was to be "by the states in their political characters." But the votes were to be "in a compound ratio," the states being treated "partly as distinct and coequal societies" and partly as unequal members of the same society. Should the duty of electing the president devolve upon the "national representatives," the representatives would vote as "individual delegations, from so many distinct and coequal bodies politic." From this aspect of the government, said Madison, it appeared "to be a mixed character, presenting at least as many federal as national features."

In the operation of its powers, the new government was, according to Madison, to be primarily a national one. He explained that the difference between a federal and a national government, as that difference related to the operations of government, was "supposed" to be that the powers of the former operated "on the political bodies composing the confederacy" while the powers of the latter operated "on the individual citizens composing the nation, in their individual capacities." When the Constitution was tested by this criterion it fell under the national and not the federal character, although not so completely as had been understood. In several respects, particularly in the trial of controversies between states, the states were to be viewed and proceeded against in their collective and political capacities only. This characteristic seemed to give the government "a few federal features."

But if the government was to be primarily national when considered from the standpoint of the operation of its powers, it was federal in respect to the extent of its powers. Its powers were to be limited and "supremacy" was to be shared with the state legislatures.

> The idea of a national government involves in it, not only an authority over the individual citizens, but an indefinite supremacy over all persons and things, so far as they are objects of lawful government. Among a people consolidated into one nation, this supremacy is completely vested in the national legislature. Among communities united for particular purposes, it is vested partly in the general and partly in the municipal legislatures. In the former case, all local authorities are subordinate to the supreme; and may be controlled, directed, or abolished by it at pleasure. In the latter, the local or municipal authorities form distinct and independent portions of the supremacy, no more subject, within their respective spheres, to the general authority, than the general authority is subject to them, within its own sphere. In this relation, then, the proposed government cannot be deemed a national one; since its jurisdiction extends to certain enumerated objects only, and leaves to the several states a residuary and inviolable sovereignty over all other objects.[52]

Lastly, Madison argued that if the Constitution was tested by its relation to the authority by which its amendment was to be accomplished it would be found to be neither wholly national nor wholly federal.

> Were it wholly national, the supreme and ultimate authority would reside in the *majority* of the people of the union; and this authority would be competent at all times, like that of a majority of every national society, to alter or abolish its established government. Were it wholly federal, on the other hand, the concurrence of each state in the union would be essential to every alteration that would be binding on all.[53]

The amending authority under the Constitution would be partly federal, both because it would represent a departure

---

[52] *Ibid.*, I, No. 39, 261-62.   [53] *Ibid.*, I, No. 39, 262-63.

from the principle of simple majority rule and because the majority actually to be required for the adoption of amendments was to be a majority of the states. But since the adoption of an amendment would not require the assent of all of the states, the amending authority would also partake of the national character.[54]

In Number 40 of the *Federalist,* Madison discussed whether the Federal Constitutional Convention had been authorized to frame and propose the Constitution. In the course of this paper, he endeavored to show that the existing Confederation and the proposed union were similar in respect to basic principles of organization. He reiterated his argument that the states were to be regarded "as distinct and independent sovereignties" in the ratification of the Constitution, and again pointed out that the members of one branch of the new government were to be chosen by the state legislatures and that the powers of the new government were in some instances to operate on states in their collective capacities. He also noted that the delegates to the Confederation Congress could be, and in two states (Connecticut and Rhode Island) actually were, chosen directly by the people. Further, he enumerated subjects in respect to which the powers of the Confederation Congress operated immediately upon individuals. In conclusion, he wrote:

> The truth is, that the great principles of the Constitution proposed by the convention may be considered less as absolutely new, than as the expansion of principles which are found in the Articles of Confederation. The misfortune under the latter system has been, that these principles are so feeble and confined as to justify all the charges of inefficiency which have been urged against it, and to require a degree of enlargement which gives to the new system the aspect of an entire transformation of the old.[55]

In his analysis of the federal and non-federal aspects of the proposed new government, Madison must be said to have paid

---

[54] *Ibid.,* I, No. 39, 263.   [55] *Ibid.,* I, No. 40, 268-69.

due respect to the common usage of the terms "federal" and "national," and perhaps the analysis served its purpose of winning support for the Constitution from some of those who had so greatly feared the growth of national power. However, Patrick Henry, for one, professed to be unconvinced by the analysis. When the Constitution was being considered by the Virginia Ratifying Convention, he commented:

> We may be amused if we please, by a treatise of political anatomy. In the brain it is national: the stamina are federal—some limbs are federal, others national. The senators are voted for by the state legislatures, so far it is federal. Individuals choose the members of the first branch; here it is national. It is federal in conferring general powers; but national in retaining them. It is not to be supported by the states—the pockets of individuals are to be searched for its maintenance. What signifies it to me, that you have the most curious anatomical description of it in its creation. To all the common purpose of legislation, it is a great consolidation of government.[56]

In the light of later controversy over the nature of the union under the Constitution, the point about the foundation of the union was more important than all of the other points covered in Madison's analysis. But the inferences that might be drawn from considering the Constitution as emanating from the people in the capacity of states were not explored during the ratification debates. It was certainly not unreasonable to assume that a document which after all was to be a compact among states fell short of fulfilling Madison's own previously evidenced desire for an instrument that would not fall into the category of treaties among nations. However, he probably did think of an assent given by the people as affording a firmer basis for union than an assent given by state legislatures, even if the assent of the people was considered to be given in the capacity of states.

[56] Elliot, III, 179-80.

Federalism and Sovereignty

The conception one had of the fundamental nature of the existing Confederation or of the union contemplated by the Constitution ultimately depended on his conception of the nature and location of sovereignty. Yet this latter conception remained so elusive that any argument based on it could immediately be made to appear defective. Not only did the meaning of the term "sovereignty" vary among different participants in the debates over the framing and ratification of the Constitution, but it also sometimes varied with the same participants. Sometimes it meant powers exercised by governmental organs and sometimes what was represented as the source of these powers. Occasionally it referred to indivisible power and at other times to power which was assumed to be capable of division.

When the Virginia plan was opposed on the ground that its adoption would mean the destruction of the sovereignty of the states, Wilson and Hamilton in effect argued that the states had never possessed full sovereignty. Both implicitly denied the validity of the assumption that the states had been thrown into a state of nature when they separated from Great Britain.[57] With Hamilton supporting his views, Wilson drew upon a doctrine which he had held as early as 1785. He had argued then that the Congress of the Confederation was authorized to charter a proposed bank of North America on the ground that the Articles of Confederation had but continued a union in existence before the Declaration of Independence and that certain powers, including the power in question, in this union from the beginning, had not been weakened or abridged by the adoption of the Articles. He stressed the point that the colonies had been referred to in the Declaration of Independence as *"these United Colonies,"* and that they had been declared to be free and independent states without being separately men-

[57] Farrand, *Records,* I, 324.

tioned.[58] They were, he stated in the Federal Convention, "independent, not *Individually* but *Unitedly*"; they "were confederated as they were independent, states."[59]

In the Federal Convention Rufus King of Massachusetts countered the argument that the states were sovereign with the assertion that the states upon entering the Confederation had divested themselves of "essential portions" of sovereignty. He pointed out that acts of the Confederation Congress were legally binding even when they were contrary to the instructions of the states to their delegates in the Congress. If the Congress declared war, that act was *de jure*, notwithstanding the wishes of the states.[60] Madison evidently intended to argue during the early proceedings of the Federal Convention that the sovereignty of the states was limited by the Articles of Confederation. The laws of the states "in relation to the paramount law of the Confederacy" were, he said, analogous to by-laws in their relation to the "supreme law" in a state. Apparently assuming a regime of law in almost every political system, he observed that there was a "gradation" from the smallest corporation with the most limited powers to the largest empire with the most perfect sovereignty.[61]

Other strong unionists in the Federal Convention, however, invoked the doctrine of indivisible sovereignty by way of emphasizing that the states must be prepared to relinquish their powers if there was to be an effective central government. Hamilton declared that the "general power" must "swallow up" the state powers if it was to preserve itself. The alternative was for it to be "swallowed up" by the state powers. Two

---

[58] James Wilson, *Works*, ed. James DeWitt Andrews (Chicago, 1896), I, 557 ff.

[59] Farrand, *Records*, I, 324.

[60] *Ibid.*, I, 323-24.

[61] *Ibid.*, I, 463-64. According to the notes taken in the Convention by Robert Yates, whose accuracy Madison later disputed, Madison said that the states had never possessed the essential rights of sovereignty, that these rights were always vested in Congress. See *ibid.*, I, 471, and III, Appendix A, cccx, cocxxxix, ccclxv, cccxci.

sovereignties, he said, could not coexist within the same limits.[62] James Wilson declared in the Convention that "either the general or the state governments must be supreme." If it was meant to establish "a national government," the states would have to submit themselves as individuals.[63] When Gouverneur Morris explained the difference between a national and a federal government he added that "in all communities there must be one supreme power and one only."[64]

But however effective the conception of indivisible sovereignty may have been in winning support for the idea of a strong union during the early debates in the Federal Convention, it could be of little if any usefulness in winning support for the Constitution as finally drafted. For the Constitution appeared on its face to be an effort to establish a system in which neither the central nor the state authorities would be supreme in anything like an absolute sense. Actually it was the opponents of the Constitution who made use of the conception of indivisible sovereignty during the ratification controversy. As used by them, the conception did not really mean that either the central or the state units had to be supreme in all matters. In fact, they apparently assumed it was feasible to establish a permanent legal division of powers if only the central government were confined to matters which were clearly of a general nature and if other matters were left to the states. But what they intended to emphasize was that the central government and a state government could not concurrently exercise jurisdiction within the same legislative areas and over the same objects without one of them emerging supreme over the other. The central government, they said, would emerge supreme. Especially would this government prove to be too strong a competitor for the state governments if it were permitted to enter the field of direct taxation, which,

[62] *Ibid.*, I, 287.
[63] *Ibid.*, I, 172.
[64] *Ibid.*, I, 34.

under the Articles of Confederation, had been reserved exclusively to the state governments.

In a pamphlet setting forth his objections to the Constitution, James Monroe insisted that state "sovereignty" would no longer exist if the central government were given the right to exercise "direct legislation within the states," holding that vesting this right in the central government would mean a "complete consolidation or incorporation of the whole into one." There was, he wrote, a maxim in government as there was in physics that two powers could not occupy the same place at the same time.[65] Later, in the Virginia Ratifying Convention, he contended that a concurrent power in the central and state governments to levy direct taxes upon the people would occasion a perpetual conflict that "must terminate to the disadvantage if not in the annihilation" of the states.[66]

The same view was supported by William Grayson and Patrick Henry in the Virginia Ratifying Convention. Grayson asked if it were not a "political absurdity" to suppose that there could be "two concurrent legislatures" each possessing the supreme power of direct taxation. If two powers came into contact, must not one of them prevail over the other? Must it not strike everyone's mind that "two unlimited, co-equal, coordinate authorities, over the same objects" could not exist together?[67] Referring to the concurrent exercise of the taxing power, Henry said that "these two co-ordinate, interfering, unlimited powers of harrassing the community" were unexampled. They were, he insisted, the visionary projects of modern politicians. He assumed that the authority of the Congress under the new Constitution would be paramount over the authority of the states and that the Congress would take

[65] James Monroe, "Some Observations on the Constitution," *The Writings of James Monroe*, ed. S. M. Hamilton (London, 1898-1903), I, Appendix I, 322.
[66] Elliot, III, 218.
[67] *Ibid.*, III, 274.

full advantage of its superior position. So heavy would be the demands of the Congress upon the sources of revenue that little revenue would be left for the states. Not enough would be left for them to defray the expenses of their internal administration. Thus Henry declared that the states would "glide imperceptibly and gradually out of existence" and that the union would naturally "terminate in a consolidation."[68]

In the New York Ratifying Convention, Melancton Smith and Thomas Tredwell advanced this same argument regarding the concurrent power of direct taxation. Smith professed to find it as difficult to conceive of two powers acting together in taxation as it was to conceive of two bodies occupying the same place. The two powers, he observed, would interfere with and be hostile toward one another.[69] Tredwell termed the "idea of two distinct sovereigns in the same country separately *possessed* of sovereign and supreme power, in the same matters, at the same time" as much an absurdity as the notion that two separate circles might be "bounded exactly" by the same circumference. What sovereignty was left to a state government, he asked, when the control of every source of revenue and the total command of the militia were given to the general government?[70]

The approaches adopted by the advocates of the Constitution in efforts to counter this line of argument varied. Although Hamilton had argued in the early proceedings of the Federal Convention that sovereignty was indivisible, he now, in the New York Ratifying Convention, declared that it was curious sophistry to hold that where there was "one supreme" there could not be "concurrent authority." It was impossible for "two supremes" to act together, he said, only when they were "aimed at each other, or at one indivisible object." Both the laws of the United States and the laws of the states were supreme as to all their respective constitutional objects. These

[68] *Ibid.*, III, 161.
[69] *Ibid.*, II, 317.
[70] *Ibid.*, II, 376.

"supreme laws" might act on different objects without clashing, and they might operate harmoniously "on different parts of the same object." Suppose, said Hamilton, both the central and state governments should levy a tax of a penny on a certain article. Did not each of the governments have an independent and uncontrollable authority to collect its own tax? The meaning of the maxim that there could not be two supremes was simply that two powers could not be supreme over each other.[71] Although Hamilton was to become, following the adoption of the Constitution, the first great champion of the doctrine that the central government possessed implied powers, he now insisted that the states were to be regarded as retaining all rights which they did not expressly grant away, minimizing at the same time the possibility of interferences between the central and state governments as they concurrently exercised jurisdiction over the same objects. That the states would have an undoubted right to levy taxes in all cases in which they were not prohibited by the Constitution he held to be founded on "the obvious and important principle in confederated governments": whatever was not "expressly given to the federal head" was reserved to the members. When government was first formed by the association of individuals, "every power of the community" was delegated because the government was to extend "to every possible object." However, when a number of "these societies" united for certain purposes, the rule was different. These people, already having delegated "their sovereignty and their powers to their several governments," could not recall them and delegate them to another government "without an express act."[72]

A second way of replying to the opponents' arguments regarding sovereignty was to take the position that sovereignty in the true sense of the term always remained in the people. This is really the position eventually taken by Madison,

[71] *Ibid.*, II, 336.　　　　　　　[72] *Ibid.*, II, 342.

without, however, explaining what corporate capacity the
American people were to have, if any, once the Constitution
went into effect. After having argued that the new union was
to be founded on the assent of these people as individuals
composing separate states, he insisted that "ultimate authority"
in this union would be in the people.[73] In the Virginia Ratifying Convention, he argued that the "concurrent collections" of
taxes were to be made practicable by the fact that the general
and state authorities were to have in the people "one common
master."[74] That these authorities would be but agents of sovereign people is also implicit in a statement by Robert R.
Livingston in the New York Ratifying Convention concerning
power vested in government. He remarked:

> They [the people] consider this state, and their general govern-
> ments, as different deposits of that power. In this view, it is of little
> moment to them, whether that portion of it, which they must, for
> their own happiness, lodge in their rulers, be invested in the state
> government, only, or shared between them and the councils of
> the union. The rights they reserve are not diminished, and prob-
> ably their liberty acquires an additional security from the divi-
> sion.[75]

James Wilson asserted in the Pennsylvania Ratifying Convention that there necessarily existed in every government a
power from which there was no appeal, and which, for that
reason, might be termed "supreme, absolute and uncontrollable."[76] This power he held to be in the people. Replying to
the argument that no sovereignty would be left in the states if
the Constitution was adopted, he remarked:

> . . . I should be very glad to know at what period the state gov-
> ernments became possessed of the supreme power. On the prin-
> ciple on which I found my arguments, and that is the principle

---

[73] The *Federalist*, I, No. 46, 321.
[74] Elliot, III, 251.
[75] *Ibid.*, II, 213.
[76] *Ibid.*, II, 405.

of this Constitution, the supreme power resides in the people. If they choose to indulge a part of their sovereign power to be exercised by the state governments, they may. If they have done it the states were right in exercising it; but if they think it no longer safe or convenient, they will resume it, or make a new distribution, more likely to be productive of that good, which ought to be our constant aim.[77]

This statement by Wilson doubtless expresses the most common of the meanings given the doctrine of popular sovereignty in the latter part of the eighteenth century. The people were the source of power, and what they had granted they could take away. The fact was, however, that the doctrine did nothing to explain how a governmental system was to operate once it was created. If the American people were to be thought of as possessing ultimate sovereignty after the adoption of the Constitution, it was but reasonable to assume that the exercise of this sovereignty would come only at widely separated intervals—when there was a general disruption in the federal system or when some far-reaching constitutional change was contemplated.

Satisfying the Need for an Umpire

If there was a danger of serious interferences between the central and state governments, as opponents of the Constitution contended, some established procedure for the settlement of jurisdictional disputes was obviously needed. How this need was to be satisfied was certainly not explained by arguing that the people possessed ultimate sovereignty over the governments. That an umpire for deciding the controversies would be indispensable if the new system was to work harmoniously appears to have been clearly seen by Monroe. He lamented in the Virginia Ratifying Convention that the Constitution as it had come from the framers did not provide for an independent agency which might settle conflicts between the central and

[77] *Ibid.*, II, 465-66.

state governments and prevent encroachments on the peoples' rights. He remarked:

> There is a division of sovereignty between the national and state governments. How far then will they coalesce together? Is it not to be supposed that there will be a conflict between them? If so, will not the members of the former combine together? Where then will be the check to prevent encroachments on the rights of the people? There is not a third essentially distinct branch to preserve a just equilibrium, or to prevent such encroachments.[78]

In the *Federalist*, Hamilton and Madison both recognized the need for a final court of appeal for the jurisdictional controversies they anticipated, although they professed to have no fear that the central government would be found encroaching on the domain of the states. Hamilton emphasized that such a tribunal would be a necessary means of preventing the states from encroaching on the central authority and of guaranteeing a uniform system of law throughout the country.[79] Madison wrote that some tribunal to decide controversies relating to the boundaries of the central and state jurisdictions was "clearly essential to prevent an appeal to the sword and a dissolution of the compact."[80]

Hamilton and Madison made it clear that they regarded the Supreme Court to be established under the Constitution as satisfying the need for a final court of appeal. Other advocates of the Constitution were not so definite, but some of them did look upon judges, either federal or state or both, as in some sense having the function of umpiring the new federal system. As a delegate in the Virginia Ratifying Convention, John Marshall observed that a law of the United States which was not warranted by any of the powers enumerated would be considered by the judges as an infringement of the Constitution which they were to guard. He said they would de-

---

[78] *Ibid.*, III, 220.
[79] The *Federalist*, I, No. 28, 148-49.
[80] *Ibid.*, I, No. 39, 262.

clare the law to be void.[81] A more elaborate statement regarding the role of the judges in keeping the central and state governments within their respective limits was made by Oliver Ellsworth in the Connecticut Ratifying Convention. He remarked:

> This Constitution defines the extent of the powers of the general government. If the general legislature should at any time overleap their limits, the judicial department is a constitutional check. If the United States go beyond their powers, if they make a law which the Constitution does not authorize, it is void; and the judicial power, the national judges, who, to secure their impartiality, are to be made independent, will declare it to be void. On the other hand, if the states go beyond their limits, if they make a law which is an usurpation upon the general government, the law is void; and upright independent judges will declare it to be so.[82]

The obvious question, of course, was whether or not it was consistent with the federal principle to permit the role of umpire to be played by one or more tribunals set up as organs of a government the extent of whose powers would often be in controversy. Curiously this question appears not to have been raised by the opponents of the Constitution; but Madison was sensible of it. After emphasizing that the general and state governments were each to be "supreme" in their respective spheres, he cautiously pointed out that it would not change "the principle of the case" to permit a tribunal established under the general government to make decisions regarding the boundary between the two jurisdictions. Like Ellsworth, he emphasized that the judges were to be impartial, noting that all the usual and most effectual precautions had been taken to secure their impartiality.[83]

---

[81] Elliot, III, 503.
[82] *Ibid.*, II, 198.
[83] The *Federalist*, I, No. 39, 262.

Conclusion

The basic conflict of the arguments over the framing and ratification of the United States Constitution was a conflict between considerations of practical necessity on the one hand and predominant political and legal conceptions on the other. The considerations of practical necessity appeared to call for a drastic constitutional change, while the predominant political and legal conceptions were on the side of efforts put forward to resist such change. The most common conception of a federal union at the time was that of a union which had been created by agreement among pre-existing political entities and which conformed generally to the institutional pattern of the existing Confederation. This conception was sufficiently firmly established for it to serve the opponents of strong union as an effective intellectual weapon. The impression which they sought to convey was that the only possible alternative to a union organized on this pattern was one whose local or regional governments would be completely subordinate to a common central government.

As the proponents of strong union, such as Hamilton, Madison and Wilson, sought to demonstrate, the country was not limited to such narrow possibilities. The system of government provided for by the Constitution was, as Madison said, of a mixed character, partly federal and partly national if the terms "federal" and "national" were to have the meanings attributed to them by those who endeavored so vigorously to prevent the Constitution's adoption. It was at least plausible to think of the governments of the system as staying within their respective spheres if only jurisdictional controversies between them were left to be decided by impartial courts. Yet the debates over ratification of the Constitution did not settle the issue of the fundamental character of the new American union. Settlement of this issue was impossible as long as there remained so many conflicting ideas of the nature of a state and of sovereignty. If the people in giving their assent to the

Constitution did so as individuals composing distinct and sovereign states, as Madison argued would be the case, did these people continue to constitute a number of sovereign states after the document went into effect? Or did they, after the document went into effect, constitute a national community partly if not wholly sovereign? These are questions which have been debated in later generations.

[The federal judges] are . . . the corps of sappers and miners, steadily working to undermine the independent rights of the states, and to consolidate all power in the hands of that government in which they have so important a freehold estate. But it is not by the consolidation, or concentration of powers, but by their distribution, that good government is effected. Were not this country already divided into states, that division must be made, that each might do for itself what concerns itself directly, and what it can so much better do than a distant authority. Every state again is divided into counties, each to take care of what lies within its local bounds; each county again into townships or wards, to manage minuter details; and every ward into farms, to be governed each by its individual proprietor. Were we directed from Washington when to sow, and when to reap, we should soon want bread. It is by this petition of cares, descending in gradation from general to particular, that the mass of human affairs may be best managed, for the good and prosperity of all.

—Thomas Jefferson, "Autobiography," *Writings* (Washington, 1903-04), I, 121-22.

The Federal Courts Versus Sovereign States

How to decide the extent of the respective jurisdictions of the central and state governments was to be one of the most troublesome of all questions in American politics after 1789. If the framers of the Constitution had meant to settle this question, they had nevertheless left much room for argument about it. It was provided in the Constitution that the federal courts would have jurisdiction in all cases in law and equity arising under the Constitution and laws of the United States, and treaties made under the authority of the United States.[1] It was further provided that the Constitution, the laws of the United States made in pursuance thereof, and the treaties made under the authority of the United States should be the supreme law of the land, and that the judges in every state should be bound thereby, anything in the constitution or laws of any state to the contrary notwithstanding.[2] But did these provisions mean that decisions of the federal courts were to override decisions of the state courts where questions regarding the extent of the powers of the central and state governments were involved? Did they, in short, mean that the United States Supreme Court was to be a tribunal of last resort, with authority to act as umpire for the federal system?

Madison's and Hamilton's statements in the *Federalist* regarding the tribunal that was to decide the boundary line be-

[1] Article III, sec. 2.   [2] Article VI.

tween the two jurisdictions[3] and the position taken by the first Congress elected under the Constitution seem definitely to imply an affirmative answer to these questions. The twenty-fifth section of the Judiciary Act passed by the first Congress provides for appeals from the highest state courts to the United States Supreme Court when the validity of a treaty or statute of the United States or an authority exercised under the United States is drawn in question and the decisions are against the contested provisions, or when a state act is questioned on the ground that it violates the Constitution, a federal statute, or a treaty, and the act has been sustained in the state courts.[4] Until the Civil War, however, the constitutionality of this section was frequently challenged.

Those who have opposed the federal courts as arbiters of the federal system have invariably appealed to the rights of the states as parties to the Constitution. On the assumption that the states are parties to the Constitution, it has been held that the states must be regarded as judges of any infractions of that document. It is noteworthy that Madison argued during the controversy over ratification of the Constitution that it was to be established by the unanimous decision of the several states that became parties to it.[5] Toward the end of the eighteenth century he insisted that the states had actually become parties to the Constitution. In the earlier period he was a unionist seeking to win support for the adoption of the Constitution; in the later period he was a Jeffersonian seeking to prevent the expansion of federal power in areas where the liberties of individuals were involved. The same doctrine served him in both instances.

The Virginia and Kentucky Resolutions

The Virginia and Kentucky Resolutions of 1798, prepared in their original drafts by Madison and Jefferson, respectively,

---

[3] See *supra*, Chap. 3, p. 86.
[4] *Statutes-at-Large of the United States* (Washington), I, 73, 85-86.
[5] See *supra*, Chap. 3, p. 73 and note.

and adopted by the legislatures of the two states, signaled the beginning of controversy over what body or bodies had power to decide finally cases involving alleged infractions of the Constitution.[6] The Resolutions were meant to be protests against the Alien and Sedition Acts passed in 1798 by a Federalist-dominated Congress, but they contained statements of much more general import. In the Virginia Resolutions Virginia's General Assembly declared that it viewed the powers of the central government as resulting from the "compact" to which the states were "parties," and that "in case of a deliberate, palpable, and dangerous exercise of other powers, not granted by the said compact," the states had the right and were in duty bound "to interpose, for arresting the progress of the evil, and for maintaining within their respective limits, the authorities, rights and liberties appertaining to them." In the Kentucky Resolutions it was declared that each state had acceded to the "compact" of union as a state and was "an integral party," that the government created by the "compact" was not made "the exclusive or final judge of the extent of the powers delegated to itself," and that "as in all other cases of compact, among private parties having no common judge, each party has an equal right to judge for itself, as well of infractions, as of the mode and measure of redress." In neither of the two sets of Resolutions were citizens formally absolved from their duty to obey the Alien and Sedition Acts, but both sets branded these Acts as unconstitutional, the Kentucky Resolutions including the declaration that the Acts were "altogether void and of no force."

The Kentucky Resolutions were based on the assumption that the states alone were parties to the Constitution, an assumption that was to be adopted quite generally by later states' rights theorists. Some difference of opinion existed among

[6] Copies of the Virginia and Kentucky Resolutions are included in *Debates in the Several State Conventions on the Adoption of the Federal Constitution*, ed. Jonathan Elliot, 2nd ed. (Washington, 1836), IV, 554-55, 566-70.

members of the Virginia legislature as to whether the states were the only parties to the Constitution or were parties along with the people as individuals. As submitted to the Virginia legislature, the Virginia Resolutions specifically stated that the states *alone* were parties,[7] but this expression was objected to on the ground that the people (presumably the people acting simply as individuals) had played a role in the adoption of the Constitution.[8] Following the objection, the word "alone" was deleted to make the Resolutions read simply that the states were parties, leaving it an open question whether they were the only parties.

Both sets of Resolutions called upon the legislatures of other states for an expression of sentiments on the constitutionality of the Alien and Sedition Acts. Nearly all of the legislatures of the Federalist-dominated northeastern states made replies condemning the doctrines of Virginia and Kentucky.[9] The position generally taken by these legislatures was that it rested with the federal courts and not with the state legislatures to decide upon the constitutionality of federal enactments. The legislature of Delaware resolved that it considered the Virginia Resolutions to be "a very unjustifiable interference with the general government and constituted authorities of the United States, and of dangerous tendency, and therefore not fit subject for the further consideration of the General Assembly."[10] The Massachusetts legislature, which was itself later to assert the right of state interposition, declared that it could not admit the right of the state legislatures to denounce the administration of that government to which the people themselves by a "solemn compact" had exclusively committed

---

[7] See the *Virginia Report of 1799-1800 Touching the Alien and Sedition Laws; together with the Virginia Resolutions of December 21, 1798, the Debate and Proceedings thereon in the House of Delegates of Virginia* (Richmond, 1850), p. 148.
[8] *Ibid.*, p. 122.
[9] Copies of many of the replies are included in *State Documents on Federal Relations*, ed. H. V. Ames (Philadelphia, 1911), pp. 16-26.
[10] *Ibid.*, p. 16.

their national concerns.[11] The House of Representatives of Pennsylvania, another state that was to change positions on the right of state interposition, resolved that it considered a declaration by a state legislature that an act of Congress was void "as a revolutionary measure, destructive of the purest principles of our state and national compacts." The House declared itself to be of the opinion that "the people of the United States" had "committed to the supreme judiciary of the nation the high authority of ultimately and conclusively deciding upon the constitutionality of all legislative acts."[12] The legislature of Vermont resolved that it belonged "not to state legislatures to decide on the constitutionality of laws made by the general government; this power being exclusively vested in the judiciary courts of the union."[13]

The replies from the other states brought rejoinders from Virginia and Kentucky. In 1799 the Kentucky legislature reaffirmed its earlier position, resolving that the several states that had formed the federal union, being "sovereign and independent," had the unquestionable right to judge of the infractions and that "a nullification by those sovereignties" of all unauthorized acts done under the color of the Constitution was the rightful remedy. However cheerfully Kentucky was disposed to surrender its opinion to a majority of its sister states in matters of ordinary or doubtful policy, it would consider silent acquiescence in momentous regulations like the Alien and Sedition Acts as highly criminal. As a party to the federal compact, it would bow to the laws of the union, but it would not cease to oppose in a constitutional manner every attempt to violate that compact.[14] In 1800 the Virginia Assembly adopted what was to be known as the Madison Report, in which it reaffirmed the position it had taken in 1798.[15] This Report, prepared by James Madison for a legislative

[11] *Ibid.*, p. 18.   [12] *Ibid.*, p. 20.
[13] *Ibid.*, p. 26.
[14] Elliot, IV, 571-72.
[15] See note 7, *supra*. The *Report* is reprinted in Elliot, IV, 572-608.

committee, consisted in a detailed examination of each of the earlier Virginia Resolutions. In support of the Resolution in which the assertion had been made that the states were parties to the Constitution and had the right of interposition, this committee entered into an examination of uses of the term "states." It was admitted that the term was "sometimes used in a vague sense, and sometimes in different senses." It sometimes meant "the separate sections of territory occupied by the political societies within each"; sometimes "the particular governments, established by those societies"; sometimes "those societies as organized into those particular governments"; and sometimes "the people composing those political societies, in their highest sovereign capacity." The Report continued:

> Although it might be wished that the perfection of language admitted less diversity in the signification of the same words, yet little inconvenience is produced by it, where the true sense can be collected with certainty from the different applications. In the present instance, whatever different construction of the term "states," in the resolution, may have been entertained, all will at least concur in that last mentioned; because, in that sense, the Constitution was submitted to the "states"; in that sense the "states" ratified it: and, in that sense of the term "states," they are consequently parties to the compact, from which the powers of the federal government result.[16]

It was stated in the Report that it appeared to the committee "to be a plain principle, founded in common sense, illustrated by common practice, and essential to the nature of compacts that, where resort can be had to no tribunal, superior to the authority of the parties, the parties themselves must be the rightful judges in the last resort, whether the bargain made has been pursued or violated." Since the states were "parties to the constitutional compact, and in their sovereign capacity," it followed of necessity that there could be no tribunal above their authority and, consequently, that they must decide in the

[16] *Ibid.*, IV, 573-74.

last resort such questions as might be "of sufficient magnitude to require their interposition."[17]

Replies from other states insisted that in the last resort the judicial authority was to be regarded as the sole expositor of the federal Constitution. To this argument the committee responded that there might be cases of usurped power which "the forms of the Constitution" would never draw within the control of the judicial department. Moreover, the committee pointed out that the Resolution of the Virginia legislature asserting the right of state interposition supposed that the judicial department might itself "exercise or sanction dangerous powers beyond the grant of the Constitution." If it were true that the judicial department had power to decide in the last resort all questions submitted to it "by the forms of the Constitution," this last resort must be deemed last in relation to the other departments of the general government. It could not mean last in relation to the rights of "the parties to the constitutional compact," from which the judicial department and the other departments held "their delegated trusts." On any other hypotheses, said the committee, the delegation of judicial power would annul the authority delegating it.[18]

The committee entered a word of caution about occasions that might seem to call for state interposition. It held that the states ought not to interpose "in a hasty manner or on doubtful and inferior occasions." Here the committee drew a lesson from the rules governing interpretations of "ordinary conventions" between nations. It recalled the "strict rule" of interpreting such conventions, according to which a breach of one provision might be deemed a breach of the whole. Even in the case of such conventions, resort to such strict interpretation was not justified unless the breach was "both wilful and material." "But in the case of an intimate and constitutional union, like that of the United States," said the committee, "it is evident that the interposition of the parties, in their sover-

17 *Ibid.*, IV, 574.   18 *Ibid.*, IV, 575-76.

eign capacity, can be called for by occasions only, deeply and essentially affecting the vital principles of their political system."[19]

The important question, of course, was what the right of state interposition was to mean. Was its meaning to be broad enough to include the constitutional right of a single state to prohibit enforcement within its borders of a federal measure regarded by the state as a palpable infringement of the federal Constitution? Presumably those condemning the Virginia and Kentucky Resolutions understood that this broad meaning had been intended. Certainly this meaning could be inferred from the Kentucky Resolutions of 1798, for they referred to the right of each state to be its own judge of the mode and measure of redress, and in the 1799 Resolutions nullification was specifically mentioned as the rightful remedy. It was also but reasonable to assume that the words "altogether void and of no force" in the Kentucky Resolutions of 1798 meant that the people of Kentucky were to disregard completely the measures to which the words referred. There are evidences, however, that the idea that a single state had the constitutional right to nullify a measure of the central government was not palatable to Madison, regardless of how palatable it might have been to Jefferson and the Kentucky legislature, or to the Virginia legislature. As a partisan along with Jefferson, Madison was doubtless ready to give any support that he could in good conscience give to what was in fact the beginning of a general campaign to oust the Federalist Party from power; and the whipping up of public sentiment by the use of inflammatory language which reflected the spirit of the American Revolution was a means toward accomplishing this end. But near the end of the Virginia Legislative Committee Report, in an effort to dispel any notion that the Virginia legislature could be charged with culpability, Madison cautioned against reading too much into the language used in the Virginia Resolu-

[19] *Ibid.*, IV, 574-75.

tions. He still defended the right of a state's legislature to make declarations denying the constitutionality of federal measures, but defended this right on the ground that these declarations were but expressions of opinion which could have no other effect than to excite reflection and thus influence other opinion. He emphasized that neither the state legislatures nor citizens, in making such declarations, were assuming the office of the judge, distinguishing judicial decisions from declarations by state legislatures and citizens by noting that the expositions of the judiciary were carried into immediate effect by force.[20] He went on to list other modes of action which had been open to the states for opposing the Alien and Sedition Acts and which he noted as being strictly within the limits of the federal Constitution. These included the making of direct representations to Congress to bring about a repeal of the two Acts; the making of efforts through established procedures to bring about an explanatory amendment to the Constitution; and the sounding of an alarm to the people informing them of usurpations on the part of the general government.[21]

Although the first part of the Legislative Committee Report contained the statement that there could be no tribunal above the authority of the "sovereign states" and that these states must therefore decide in the last resort questions of sufficient magnitude to require their interposition, there is a general consistency between the latter part of this report and a statement by Madison in 1830 in which he rejected as untenable the doctrine that a single state had the constitutional right to nullify a federal measure. In both cases his references, in discussing action to be taken against unauthorized federal measures, were usually to what the *states* might do rather than to what a single state might do. He denied in 1830 that the Virginia legislature had in 1798 intended to sanction the doctrine that a single state had the constitutional right of nullification, explaining that concert among the states for redressing the

<hr>

[20] *Ibid.*, IV, 605-06.   [21] *Ibid.*, IV, 606-07.

Alien and Sedition Acts had been a leading sentiment in the Virginia House of Delegates when the Virginia Resolutions were being debated. He went on to state that the immediate object had been to invite the other states to concur in declaring the Alien and Sedition Acts unconstitutional and to co-operate by necessary and proper measures in maintaining unimpaired the authorities, rights, and liberties reserved to the states and to the people. It could not be doubted, he wrote, that the necessary and proper measures to be taken had meant "measures known to the Constitution, particularly the ordinary control of the people and legislatures of the states, over the government of the United States."[22] Madison still subscribed to the notion that a state might in certain circumstances be justified in appealing to "original rights and the law of self-preservation." This was the *"ultima ratio"* under all governments, whether they were consolidated, were confederated, or were a compound of both. But the right to make this appeal was not a constitutional right but an extra- and ultra-constitutional right. It was to be resorted to only when there had been an accumulation of usurpations and abuses rendering passive obedience and non-resistance a greater evil than resistance and revolution and when all possible constitutional remedies had failed.[23]

Other Protests in the Jeffersonian Era

While Madison's statements near the end of the Virginia legislative committee report of 1800 make the Virginia Resolutions appear innocuous enough, it is nevertheless true that this report and the Virginia and Kentucky Resolutions suggested a line of approach which was to be followed in innumerable later protests against exercises of federal power. For this reason these several documents are unsurpassed in importance by any other writings in American particularist literature. As will be

[22] *North American Review*, XXXI, Pt. II (1830), 537, 545.
[23] *Ibid.*, XXXI, Pt. II, 542.

noted shortly, the general theory of the nature of the American union which was suggested in the Resolutions and in the first part of the report was elaborately developed by Jeffersonian writers in the first quarter of the nineteenth century. However, Jeffersonians, who were in control of the executive and legislative branches of the central government for nearly the entire period, were by no means the only ones to resort to and draw significant implications from the doctrine that the United States Constitution was a compact to which the states were parties. Various groups employed this doctrine, frequently using it to oppose even federal measures for which the presidential administrations of Jefferson and Madison were at least primarily responsible. Some of the strongest protests against measures of the executive and legislative branches of the central government during the administrations of Jefferson and Madison came from New England, where the Federalist Party continued to predominate and where commercial interests felt the crippling effects of federal embargo legislation and the War of 1812. The protest movement culminated near the end of the War in the assembling of the Hartford Convention, whose primary objective was to find ways to strengthen the position of the states in the union. The clearest statements about the nature of the union to grow out of this movement are to be found in certain of the resolutions and committee reports of the several state legislatures of the section. Particularly important in this connection are resolutions and committee reports relating to the admission into the union of states organized in territories acquired after the adoption of the Constitution, to the embargo acts, and to the calling of state militia into the service of the United States.

A position taken in Massachusetts was that those who framed and ratified the Constitution had not intended that the political weight of the states in the union be diminished by the admission of new states carved out of territory acquired after the Constitution's ratification. In a report of 1813 a committee of this state's legislature declared:

The proportion of the political weight of each foreign state, composing this union, depends upon the number of the states, which have a voice under the compact. This number, the Constitution permits Congress to multiply, at pleasure, within the limits of the original states, observing, only, the expressed limitations in the Constitution. To pass these limitations and admit states, beyond the ancient boundaries, is . . . an usurpation, as dangerous as it is manifest, inasmuch as these exterior states, after being admitted on an equal footing with the original states, may, and as they multiply, certainly will become, in fact, the arbiters of the destinies of the nation; by availing themselves of the contrariety of interests and views which in such a confederacy of states necessarily arise, they hold the balance among the respective parties and govern the states, constitutionally composing the union, by throwing their weight into whatever scale is most conformable to the ambition or projects of such foreign states.[24]

The chairman of the committee that made the report was Josiah Quincy. Two years earlier, as a member of the United States House of Representatives, he had made an impassioned speech against the organization of the territory of Orleans into a state. In this speech he declared it to be his deliberate opinion that the passage of the bill to organize the territory into a state would itself virtually constitute a dissolution of the union. He declared that the states would be free from their moral obligations and that it would be the right of all, and the duty of some, to prepare for a separation, amicably if they could, but "violently if they must."[25]

The legislatures of Massachusetts, Connecticut, and Rhode Island all passed resolutions condemning the embargo legislation and asserting that Congress had exceeded its constitutional authority in passing it. In Rhode Island a legislative committee on the embargo reported that the people of the state, "as one of the parties to the federal compact," had a right to ex-

[24] Ames, p. 67.
[25] *Annals of the Congress of the United States,* 11th Cong., 3d sess., col. 525.

press their sense of any violation of the compact's provisions, and that it was the duty of the state's legislature, as the organ of the peoples' sentiments and the depository of their power, to interpose for the purpose of protecting them from the ruinous inflictions of usurped and unconstitutional power.[26] The Massachusetts legislature reacted to the embargo legislation by adopting a legislative committee report which asserted the right of a state to interpose for protecting its citizens against illegal exercises of power by the general government.

> We spurn the idea that the free, sovereign and independent State of Massachusetts is reduced to a mere municipal corporation, without power to protect its people, and to defend them from oppression, from whatever quarter it comes. Whenever the national compact is violated, and the citizens of this state are oppressed by cruel and unauthorized laws, this legislature is bound to interpose its power, and wrest from the oppressor its victim.
>
> This is the spirit of our union, and thus has it been explained by the very man [presumably President Madison], who now sets at defiance all the principles of his early political life.[27]

Several New England states raised protests during the War of 1812 against the calling of the militia of the states into the service of the United States without the consent of state authorities, taking the position that the states had the right to determine when exigencies warranted the use of the state militia in federal service.[28] In a report on the subject adopted by the Connecticut legislature, it was declared that:

> . . . It must not be forgotten, that the state of Connecticut is a free sovereign and independent state; that the United States are a *confederacy* of states; that we are a confederated and not a consolidated republic. The governor of this state is under a high and solemn obligation, "*to maintain the lawful rights and privileges thereof as a sovereign, free and independent state,*" as he is "*to support the constitution of the United States,*" and the obligation to support the latter, imposes an additional obligation to

---

[26] Ames, pp. 43-44.   [27] *Ibid.*, pp. 71-72.
[28] *Ibid.*, pp. 54 ff.

support the former. The building cannot stand, if the pillars upon which it rests are impaired or destroyed.[29]

A state outside of New England where the issue of state sovereignty versus federal power was repeatedly raised in the decade and a half immediately following the adoption of the Virginia and Kentucky Resolutions was Pennsylvania. While these Resolutions were still being hotly debated, this state's Supreme Court relied on the doctrine that the states were parties to the United States Constitution in support of the Court's denial of a petition for transfer of a case from its docket to a federal circuit court. Taking the position that there was aside from the people no "common umpire" between the central and state governments for controversies relating to their respective jurisdictions, the state Court said:

> In such a case, the Constitution of the United States is federal; it is a league or treaty, made by the individual states, as one party, and all the states, as another party. When two nations differ about the meaning of any clause, sentence or word in a treaty, neither has an exclusive right to decide it; they endeavor to adjust the matter by negotiation, but if it cannot be thus accomplished, each has a right to retain its own interpretation, until a reference be had to the mediation of other nations, an arbitration, or the fate of war.[30]

The Court viewed the federal Constitution as defective in that it did not provide for a tribunal to decide cases of conflicts between the central and state governments over their respective jurisdictions. It regarded the United States Supreme Court as neither legally competent nor a suitable agency to decide such cases, suggesting that the vice-president and Senate of the United States, or a commission of one member from each state, might be a "more proper tribunal" than the Supreme Court.[31]

Over a period of years, the Pennsylvania legislature sought, by threats to resort to military force and otherwise, to prevent

[29] *Ibid.,* p. 61.
[30] *Respublica* v. *Cobbett,* 3 Dallas (Pa.) 467, 473-74 (1798).
[31] *Ibid.,* p. 474.

the enforcement of a federal court decree in the case of Gideon Olmstead. The legislature took the position that the case did not come within the federal courts' jurisdiction. Eventually in *United States* v. *Peters*, which involved the Olmstead case, the United States Supreme Court, speaking through Chief Justice Marshall, denied that a state legislature had a right to determine the jurisdiction of the federal courts.[32] However, the decree in question was enforced only after a federal posse of 2,000 men had been summoned. In resolutions adopted by the legislature, it was lamented that the federal Constitution did not provide for an impartial tribunal to decide cases of disputed jurisdiction between the central and state governments. The state's senators and representatives in Congress were called upon to use their influence toward the procuring of a constitutional amendment that would provide for such a tribunal.[33]

Pennsylvania protested against a renewal of the charter of the Bank of the United States in 1811 on the ground that the central government had not been delegated the authority to grant charters of incorporation within the jurisdiction of a state without the state's consent. In resolutions of the General Assembly of the State it was asserted:

> The people of the United States by the adoption of the federal Constitution established a general government for special purposes, reserving to themselves respectively, the rights and authorities not delegated in that instrument. To the compact thereby created, each state acceded in its character as a state, and is a party. The act of union thus entered into being to all intents and purposes a treaty between sovereign states, the general government by this treaty was not constituted the exclusive or final judge of the powers it was to exercise; for if it were so to judge then its judgment and not the Constitution would be the measure of its authority.
>
> Should the general government in any of its departments vio-

[32] 5 Cranch 115, 136 (1809).
[33] For full details concerning the Olmstead case see William O. Douglas, "United States v. Peters, 5 Cranch 115," *Federal Rules Decisions*, XIX (1956), 185-94, and Ames, pp. 45-52.

late the provisions of the Constitution, it rests with the states, and with the people to apply suitable remedies.[34]

As the United States Supreme Court under the leadership of Chief Justice John Marshall in effect established itself as umpire of the American federal system its suitability and legal competence for this role came more and more to be disputed by Jeffersonian leaders. The legislature of Virginia signified its approval of this role for the Court when, following the decision in the Olmstead case, the legislature of Pennsylvania made its proposal for a constitutional amendment providing for an "impartial tribunal."[35] However, following the Court's acceptance in the case of *McCulloch* v. *Maryland* of the doctrine that the federal Constitution granted implied powers to Congress,[36] a paper was submitted for adoption by the Virginia legislature in which it was declared that

> In those great and important contests, which may arise upon the true construction of the compact, it must devolve on the parties, themselves, to judge of the infractions of it, whether occasioned by the legislature, the executive, or the judiciary.—This results from the plain consideration that the parties to the federal compact were sovereign states, and that, with respect to the powers retained, the states are as sovereign as the United States are, as to those granted.—It could never therefore have been the intention of the states to submit the extent of their authorities, and rights, to courts created by one party to the compact, which party has the *appointment of judges;* who, however enlightened and honest, *could* not be *presumed,* in a contest between *rival* authorities, to be *exempt* from the *esprit de corps,* to which all men may be, more or less, subject; and, who in relation to the diminution of duties, and *increase of compensation,* at least, are dependent on the very body whose acts, or authority, may be brought in question.[37]

[34] *Ibid.,* p. 53.
[35] *Annual Report of the American Historical Association for 1896* (Washington, 1897), II, 160, note 3.
[36] 4 Wheaton 316 (1819).
[37] *Niles' Weekly Register,* XVII (1820), 312.

The paper, which was intended to instruct the senators from Virginia in Congress, called for efforts to bring about an amendment to the Constitution for the creation of a new tribunal to decide questions in which the powers and authorities of the general and state governments were in conflict. It was perceived that questions of great delicacy and importance might arise between "the parties to the compact,"—questions which ought to be referred to a tribunal not appointed exclusively by the states or the general government in order to insure public confidence and reconcile jarring and conflicting interests. Such a tribunal might be exempt from feelings which, however honest, might militate against an unbiased decision.[38]

This idea of a new tribunal harmonized with Jefferson's views regarding the federal judiciary as expressed in his later years. In his "Autobiography" he expressed a desire to see the federal judges subjected to "some practical and impartial control," emphasizing among other points that the judges were too much a part of the central government. He explained that the control desired would, in order to be "imparted," have to be "compounded of a mixture of state and federal authorities."[39]

There were strong protests in Virginia against the calling of the state before the United States Supreme Court in the case of *Cohens* v. *Virginia*.[40] In a committee report adopted by the House of Delegates, the conclusion was reached that there was no rightful power in the federal judiciary "to arraign the sovereignty of a commonwealth before any tribunal, but that which resides in the majesty of the people." The doctrine that the federal Constitution was a compact among sovereign states was advanced in support of this conclusion. Each of the thirteen American colonies, it was argued, had become "a perfect independent nation" when independence was secured from the mother country. As independent nations they had entered into

[38] *Ibid.*, XVII, 314.
[39] Thomas Jefferson, *Writings,* library ed. (Washington, 1903-04), I, 120-21.
[40] 6 Wheaton 264 (1821).

"two distinct confederations" by which they had surrendered certain specified national rights, while retaining their other rights. The general government, "having no original primitive rights antecedent to the federal compact, and being wholly made up of the voluntary cessions by the states," was "the mere creature of the national specified powers ceded by the states."[41]

In 1821 the state of Ohio contested the assumption that federal courts had the exclusive right to act as last resort expositors of the federal Constitution. Disregarding the holding in *McCulloch* v. *Maryland* that states had no right to tax the second Bank of the United States, Ohio officials sought to collect a state-imposed prohibitive tax on the Bank's Ohio branches.[42] Furthermore, the Ohio legislature resolved that

> In respect to the powers of the governments of the several states that compose the American union and the powers of the federal government, this General Assembly do recognize and approve the doctrines asserted by the legislatures of Kentucky and Virginia in their resolutions of November and December, 1798, and January, 1800, and do consider that their principles have been recognized and adopted by a majority of the American people.[43]

The adoption of this Resolution was recommended by a joint legislative committee, which argued in its report to the legislature that the victory of the Jeffersonian Republicans in the elections of 1800 was to be interpreted as an endorsement by the country of the doctrines of the Virginia and Kentucky Resolutions.[44]

The Jeffersonian Writers

The Jeffersonian writers of the first quarter of the nineteenth century who, in addition to Madison, deserve special attention

---

[41] *Niles' Weekly Register*, XX (March-Sept., 1821), 118-24, at pp. 119-20, 124.
[42] Ames, p. 93.   [43] *Ibid.*, p. 100.
[44] *Ibid.*, pp. 95-96.

are the three Virginians St. George Tucker, Spencer Roane, and John Taylor. Tucker, a onetime professor of law and for many years a judge, first of the Virginia state courts and later of the United States District Court for Virginia, set forth his views in an appendix to an edition of Blackstone's *Commentaries* which he published in 1803. He did not address himself in this appendix to the specific question of how jurisdictional disputes between the central authority and the members of a federal system should be settled, but he did deal in some detail with general characteristics of "confederacies." His discussion was documented by citations of the writings of half a dozen or more foreign authors, and it included some comment on the federal systems of ancient Greece and modern Europe, as well as on the American union. However, he relied chiefly, insofar as foreign sources were concerned, on Emmerich de Vattel's *Le Droit des Gens, ou Principes de la Loi Naturelle*, first published in 1758, and Samuel Pufendorf's *De Jure Naturae et Gentium*, first published in 1688.[45] Tucker held, as did Vattel, that states that united to form a "confederacy" continued to be perfect states. In Tucker's words, "two states, notwithstanding such treaties, are separate bodies and independent." The states were but "politically united" when some one person or council was constituted "with a right to exercise some essential powers for both, and to hinder either from exercising them separately."[46]

On the subject of the powers of the central authority in a "confederacy," Tucker did not deviate from Pufendorf, many of whose statements he either quoted or paraphrased. Pufendorf had written that the central "council" could exercise only such powers as were delegated from the member states, that

[45] Other writers quoted or cited by Tucker in his discussion of federal systems were Jean Barbeyrac, Sir William Blackstone, Jean Jacques Burlamaqui, and Baron de Montesquieu.

[46] See Tucker's *Blackstone's Commentaries* (Philadelphia, 1803), I, Pt. I, Appendix, 64, and Vattel's *The Law of Nations or the Principles of Natural Law*, trans. Charles G. Fenwick (Classics of International Law) (Washington, 1916), III, 12.

the state "deputies" to this council were "no more than ministers of the allies," and that these deputies could no more enjoin anything upon the "allies" with authority than an ambassador could give orders to his master.[47] Tucker wrote:

> How far the power of this council of delegates extends, is to be gathered from the words of the compact itself, or from the warrant under which they act. This is certain; that the power whatever it be, is not their own, but derived to them from those whom they represent, and although the decrees, which they publish, pass solely under their own name, yet the whole force and authority of them flows from the states, themselves, by whose consent such a council hath been erected: so that the deputies are no more than ministers of the confederate states, and are altogether as unable to enjoin any thing by their own proper authority, as an ambassador is to command and govern his master.[48]

Tucker named four causes of the dissolution of a confederacy: (1) It might be abandoned by mutual consent, or some of the member states might voluntarily withdraw. (2) Because of some accident or lack of consent among the confederate states, the legislature or executive authority of the "federal government" might be suspended. If a majority of the states refused to choose representatives or a "president" failed to be chosen at the proper time, the administration of the government would be "wholly suspended," resulting perhaps in a dissolution. (3) Intestine wars could permanently dissolve the union unless it was revived after the conclusion of peace. (4) A conqueror might seize one or more of the member states.[49] The first, third, and fourth of these causes are almost identical with three named by Pufendorf,[50] but to substantiate a right of states to withdraw from a confederacy Tucker relied on Vattel and on the doctrines of the American Declaration of Independence.

[47] Samuel Pufendorf, *De Jure Naturae et Gentium,* trans. C. H. and W. A. Oldfather (Classics of International Law) (Washington, 1916), II, 1049.
[48] Tucker, I, Pt. I, Appendix, 72-73.
[49] *Ibid.,* I, Pt. I, Appendix, 73 ff.
[50] Pufendorf, II, 1051.

He followed Vattel in holding that a state had the right to do whatever was necessary to preserve its existence as a state.[51] Then, citing the Declaration of Independence, he wrote:

> Prudence, indeed, will dictate, that governments established by compact should not be changed for light or transient causes; but should a long train of abuses and usurpations, pursuing invariably the same object, evince a design in any one of the confederates to usurp a dominion over the rest, or, if those who are intrusted to administer the government, which the confederates have for their mutual convenience established, should manifest a design to invade their sovereignty, and extend their own power beyond the terms of compact, to the detriment of the states respectively, and to reduce them to a state of obedience, and finally to establish themselves in a state of permanent superiority, it then becomes not only the right, but the duty of the states respectively, to throw off such government, and to provide new guards for their future security.[52]

Tucker appears to have regarded what he said about the status of the members and the central authorities of confederacies in general as applicable in the full sense of the term to the union under the United States Constitution. He repeatedly referred to this union as a confederacy, and it was definitely not his purpose to distinguish it from other federalized systems. His comments on the Constitution, however, could hardly be regarded as giving much support to an assumption that the states within the union were perfect states. He declared that the Constitution was a "federal compact," and also "to a certain extent, a social compact." He explained that it had had its commencement with "the body politic of the several states" and that its final adoption and ratification had been "by the several legislatures referred to and completed by conventions, especially called and appointed for the purpose in each state." The acceptance of the Constitution was "not only an act of the body politic of each state, but of the people thereof respectively, in

---

[51] Vattel, III, 14, and Tucker, I, Pt. I, 74.
[52] Tucker, I, Pt. I, 75.

their sovereign character and capacity." By it the several states and the people thereof, respectively, had bound themselves "to each other, and to the federal government of the United States," and by it the federal government was bound "to the several states, and to every citizen of the United States."[53] But if the Constitution was to be regarded as something more than a compact among states, as these statements seem to imply, how could a member of the union claim full sovereignty and how could the organs and functionaries of the central government be deemed nothing more than the states' agencies or deputies? Tucker himself recalled that the Constitution had been objected to at the time of its ratification on the ground that the people's participation in the ratification process would make the proposed new government a consolidated government. He then quoted Madison's long statement in the *Federalist* on the nature of the proposed new government which was meant to answer this objection.[54] In this statement Madison had said that the assent of the people was to be given by them, not as individuals composing an entire nation but as composing distinct and separate states. But even while quoting this statement, Tucker apparently thought of the states not as being identical with the people but as being identical with the state governmental institutions.

Tucker's lack of precision in discussing the nature of the Constitution, however, probably did not lessen his influence in spreading abroad the notion that the members of any federal system were perfect states, a notion which was to be resorted to frequently in subsequent years of the nineteenth century. In this connection it should be remarked that his edition of Blackstone's *Commentaries* was for decades an important reference work for lawyers. One of the most important attributes of the edition was that it made readily available not only Tucker's views on federal systems but also those of Vattel and Pufendorf.

53 *Ibid.*, I, Pt. I, Appendix, 140, 144, 169.
54 *Ibid.*, I, Pt. I, Appendix, 144 ff.

One of the most severe critics of the United States Supreme Court in the first quarter of the nineteenth century was Judge Spencer Roane of the Virginia Court of Appeals. In a forceful opinion in the case of *Hunter* v. *Martin* in 1814,[55] Roane joined his colleagues on the Virginia bench in refusing to obey a mandate of the United States Supreme Court reversing a decision of the state Court. He criticized the Supreme Court's decision in the case of *McCulloch* v. *Maryland* in two series of papers which he published in the *Richmond Enquirer* under the pen names Amphictyon and Hampden. He delivered another strong attack upon the Supreme Court following that Court's decision in the case of *Cohens* v. *Virginia*. Again he published a series of papers in the *Enquirer*, this time using the pen name Algernon Sidney.[56]

Both as judge and in his published articles, Roane denied that the Supreme Court was legally competent or suitable for deciding cases of disputed jurisdiction between the central and state governments. He "humbly" believed that the states never could have committed "an act of such egregious folly as to agree that their umpire should be altogether appointed and paid by the other party." The Court might be "a perfectly impartial tribunal to decide between two states," but it could never be considered "in that point of view" when the contest lay between the United States and one of its members.[57]

On the subject of the suitability of the Court for deciding cases involving jurisdictional disputes between the central and state governments, Roane invoked Vattel. He credited Vattel with the statements that it was proper for the head and members "of a confederacy" to establish an umpire or arbitrator for their disputes and that the head itself was competent to decide troubles that existed among the members. Because the head was

---

[55] 4 Mumford (Va.) 1, 25.
[56] Collections of the three series of papers mentioned appear in *The John P. Branch Historical Papers of Randolph-Macon College* (1904), pp. 357-73; (1905), pp. 51-121; and (1906), pp. 78-183. Hereinafter *Branch Historical Papers.*
[57] *Ibid.* (1905), pp. 56-57.

an interested party, it did not have jurisdiction in disputes between itself and the members, but conversely, it did have jurisdiction in disputes between members.[58] According to Roane, the United States Constitution had "gone by this principle, in both its aspects." The Constitution had expressly invested the Supreme Court with jurisdiction to decide controversies between two or more states, but it had not given it a jurisdiction over "its own controversies" with a state or states.[59]

In his analysis of the nature of the American union, Roane followed closely the reasoning of the first part of Madison's Virginia Legislative Committee Report of 1800, quoting at the same time from numerous other sources. He viewed the reference of the Constitution to popularly chosen state conventions for its ratification as constituting a reference "to the states themselves in their highest political and sovereign authority." The conventions had adopted the Constitution and brought it into existence, and they had represented "the people only within the limits of the respective sovereign states" and "not the whole mass of the population of the United States." "The individuality of the several states was still kept up when they assembled in convention: their sovereignty was still preserved, and the only effect of the adoption of the Constitution was to take from one set of their agents and servants, to wit: the state governments, a certain portion of specified powers, and to delegate that same portion to another set of servants and agents, then newly-created, namely, the federal government."[60]

The fact that the federal government had been established by action of the people of the states rather than by action of the state governments did not make it any less a federal government. The old Confederation had indeed been brought into existence by action of the state legislatures, but the validity of that action was open to question. It had taken place in the infancy of the "Republic," when the people of the country had not emancipated themselves from the opinion, still prevailing in

[58] *Ibid.* (1905), p. 119.   [59] *Ibid.* (1905), pp. 119-20.
[60] *Ibid.* (1905), p. 54. See also p. 107.

Europe, that the sovereignty of states abided "in their kings, or *governments*." But this opinion was now in this country "an outrageous heresy." None but the people of a state was competent to make or reform governments, which were deputies of the people for limited and defined objects. It was a principle of common sense, as well as of common law, that a deputy could not make a deputy. The power of "changing the government," therefore, remained with the people; thus, to say that there could be no federal government unless it was adopted by the governments of the several states was to say that there could be no federal government at all.[61]

In support of his classification of the central government as a federal government as opposed to a "sole and consolidated government," Roane quoted from Vattel, Montesquieu, and the *Federalist*. From Vattel he quoted the statement that several states might unite to form a perpetual confederacy without themselves ceasing to be perfect states.[62] From Montesquieu he quoted the famous sentence in which the Lycian confederacy had been praised as " 'a model of an excellent confederate republic.' " This quotation was meant to emphasize that, although certain features of the central government of the United States were commonly associated with consolidated governments, this government was still federal. Roane called attention to Montesquieu's description of the Lycian confederacy as an association in which a common council appointed the local judges and magistrates and in which the "towns," unequally represented, paid into the common treasury according to their ratio of representation.[63] From the *Federalist* he quoted the statement in which Hamilton had argued that where the members of a confederate republic continued to exist "of constitutional necessity" there was in fact and in theory an association of states or a confederacy. Also he quoted from Madison's essay in the *Federalist* in which the government pro-

---

[61] *Ibid.* (1905), pp. 109-10.
[62] *Ibid.* (1906), p. 99; *Hunter* v. *Martin,* 4 Mumford (Va.) 30.
[63] *Branch Historical Papers* (1905), p. 110.

vided for by the Constitution was represented as having as many federal as national features.[64]

From the various "principles and authorities" to which he referred, Roane concluded that the central government of the United States could not be considered a consolidated government either in consequence of its mode of adoption or in consequence of its having some national features. It was a *"federal* government, with some features of nationality." It was "as much a federal government, or a 'league,' as was the former Confederation." The only difference between the older Confederation and the new government was that the powers of the latter had been "much *extended."* Supporting his statement with appropriate quotations from Madison, Roane declared that the new government might "in some sense" be considered a continuation of the *"former* federal government."[65]

Roane asked: "If, then, everything conspires to show that our government is a *confederal* and not a consolidated one, how far can a state be bound by acts of the general government violating, to its injury, rights guaranteed to it, by the federal compact?" Without giving a direct answer to this question, he declared that if the founders of the Constitution had not foreseen the clashings between the governments within the American union and had not provided an impartial tribunal to decide between these governments, this only afforded another instance of the imperfection of the instrument of which its authors themselves were sensible. More than half a dozen authorities were quoted by him to support the proposition that neither the central government nor any of its departments had a right to act as the final interpreter of the Constitution and that the states had a right to interpose their authority when the central government or any of its departments assumed powers not granted to them by the Constitution. He made the assumption that the right of state interposition was supported in the *Federalist,* observing that the authors of the *Federalist* had said

[64] *Ibid.* (1905), pp. 111-12; (1906), pp. 97-98.
[65] *Ibid.* (1905), pp. 112-13.

that the states were to be expected to sound alarms and erect barriers against "encroachments of the national authority."[66] He also quoted at some length from Madison's Report of 1800, with specific reference to the role of the federal judiciary and to the right of state interposition.[67]

Of the three writers whose views on federalism are here analyzed, the one most deserving of the distinction of being an expounder of the principles of Jeffersonian democracy is John Taylor, commonly referred to as John Taylor of Caroline to associate him with the Virginia county in which he lived.[68] In his books Taylor defended individualism, localism, and agrarianism against the liberal interpretation of the Constitution which was adopted first by leaders of the Federalist Party, like Hamilton, and then by the federal courts. Taylor viewed federalism largely in terms of the purposes which it served, one of the most important being that of harnessing power to avoid the excesses to which governments were prone. Thus federalism for him provided, or was supposed to provide, one of the main dimensions of the system of checks and balances in American government. His theory of federalism therefore definitely went beyond the legalism which was so characteristic of the writings of Tucker and Roane. Nevertheless, he did not fail, in defending the right of the states in the American union, to make full use of the legal conceptions which were available to him.

Taylor's views on the nature of the union were elaborated principally in three books by him which were published in the early 1820's.[69] Much earlier than this, however, he was a leading

---

[66] *Ibid.* (1905), p. 114.   [67] *Ibid.* (1905), pp. 115-16.

[68] On Taylor as an expounder of Jeffersonian principles, see Benjamin F. Wright, "The Philosopher of Jeffersonian Democracy," *American Political Science Review*, XXII (1928), 870-92, and E. T. Mudge, *The Social Philosophy of John Taylor of Caroline* (New York, 1939). The latter work is a valuable aid for studying Taylor's political and social theory in its entirety.

[69] The three books are *Construction Construed, and Constitutions Vindicated* (Richmond, 1820); *Tyranny Unmasked* (Washington, 1822); and *New Views of the Constitution of the United States* (Washington, 1823).

exponent of the doctrine that the union had originated in a compact among the states. Four and a half months before the Kentucky Resolutions were introduced in the Kentucky legislature, he wrote Jefferson that "the right of the state governments to expound the Constitution, might possibly be made the basis of a movement towards its amendment." If this was insufficient, "the people in state conventions" were "incontrovertibly the contracting parties," and, "possessing the infringing rights," they might "proceed by orderly steps to attain the object."[70] Although Madison prepared the original draft of the Virginia Resolutions, Taylor introduced them in the Virginia legislature and led in the debate on them. In this debate Taylor did not deny that the people as individuals were parties to the Constitution, but he argued that the states were parties and that as parties they were justified "in preserving their rights under the compact against violation." Even if the framers of the Constitution had chosen to use the style " 'we the people,' " it was well known that in every step of the proceedings on the document's formation and adoption the sense of the people had appeared "through the medium of some representative state assembly, either legislative or constituent."[71]

Taylor considered it incorrect to refer to the American union as a state. There were many states in America, but there was no "state of America."[72] "A people of each state [had been] created by the Declaration of Independence, invested with sovereignty, and therefore entitled to unite or not."[73] The United States possessed no "innate sovereignty." It was not "self-constituted" but "conventional," and, of course, subordinate to the sovereignties by which it was formed.[74] The "federal" was not a "national" government; it was "a league

[70] John Taylor to Thomas Jefferson, June 25, 1798 in *Branch Historical Papers* (1908), 276.
[71] See the *Virginia Report of 1799-1800 Touching the Alien and Sedition Laws; together with the Virginia Resolutions of December 21, 1798, the Debate and Proceedings thereon in the House of Delegates of Virginia* (Richmond, 1850), p. 120.
[72] *New Views of the Constitution*, pp. 171-72.
[73] *Ibid.*, p. 8.   [74] *Ibid.*, p. 37.

between nations.''[75] The Articles of Confederation and the United States Constitution were both ratified by the separate peoples of the states, and no people of the United States was ever created.[76]

Sovereignty was referred to by Taylor as being by its nature a unit.[77] Moreover, he considered it to be an accepted principle in the United States that ultimate sovereignty was possessed by the people. "Our maxim" was that a government was "not a sovereign, but a trustee of the sovereignty of the people, invested only with limited powers and composed of coordinate departments established to discharge specific duties."[78] But the people of the United States who possessed sovereignty were the people of each state, not the people of the United States considered as one people.[79]

Without explaining clearly the implications for the union of his doctrine that sovereignty was a unit, Taylor in effect ruled out all possibility of a middle ground between "a nation consolidated under one sovereignty" and a federal union or "league" of states. The rights of a people were indivisible, and therefore one people could not exist within another.

> Common consent is necessary to constitute a people, and no such consent, expressly or impliedly, can be shewn, by which all the inhabitants of the United States have ever constituted themselves into one people. This could not have been effected without destroying every people constituted within each state, as one political being called a people cannot exist within another.
>
> The rights of a people are indivisible; and if a great people be compounded of several smaller nations, as it inherently possesses the right of self-government, it must absorb the same right of self-government in its component parts; just as the rights of individuals are absorbed by the communities into which they constitute themselves. Therefore had a people been constituted, by melting down the little nations into one great nation, those little

---

[75] *Construction Construed*, p. 234.
[76] *Ibid.*, p. 46, and *New Views of the Constitution*, pp. 12 ff.
[77] *Construction Construed*, pp. 27, 114.   [78] *Ibid.*, p. 264.
[79] *New Views of the Constitution*, p. 79.

nations must have lost the right of self-government, because they would no longer have been a people.[80]

That the American states had a right to withdraw from their federal union Taylor regarded as not open to question. In creating the federal government the states had exercised "the highest act of sovereignty," and they might if they pleased "repeat the proof of their sovereignty by its annihilation." The sovereignties which had imposed limitations on the central government had reserved powers in which this government could not participate, and they had reserved "the usual right of sovereigns to alter or revoke its commissions."[81]

The idea that the federal courts should be regarded as tribunals of last resort in expounding the federal Constitution was wholly unacceptable to Taylor. Implicitly he argued that any branch of the central government with an absolute negative over the states would destroy the federal character of the union. "If one part of the federal sphere possessed a supreme negative over the acts of all parts of the state spheres, the sovereignty and independence allowed to the latter, would be as completely destroyed, as if the entire state spheres were thus subjected to the entire federal sphere." If the judiciaries of the states were made subject to the judicial branch of the federal government, the "residuary and inviolable sovereignty" of the states, "both legislative and judicial," would be annihilated.[82]

The states had a power to veto unconstitutional laws, a power of the same nature as that of the federal judges, who had never been expressly granted such authority. Being at least as much "political departments" as the courts of justice, the states derived from this characteristic the same power to reject unconstitutional laws that the judges had. "In other views" the states' right of rejection was infinitely the strongest.

As contracting parties to the union, this right [to reject unconstitutional laws] is an appendage of that character. If they are not to be so considered, it goes to them as representatives of the peo-

[80] *Construction Construed*, pp. 46-47.
[81] *New Views of the Constitution*, p. 37.   [82] *Ibid.*, p. 114.

ple, because it is an appendage of the political power with which they are invested by the people. It is absurd to allow that they were intrusted by the Constitution with these powers, and yet prohibited from looking themselves into the Constitution, that they might exercise them faithfully. The states possessed political powers antecedent to the Constitution, as is acknowledged by their reservation. These state political powers previously possessed, never surrendered and expressly retained, inherently comprise a moral right of self-defense against every species of aggression; and the Constitution, instead of saying that they may be taken away by the federal government, expressly declares that they shall not; that they are without the compass of that instrument and not embraced by it at all. Here then is a positive constitutional veto, clearly precluding both Congress and the federal courts from touching the reserved state rights.[83]

Although Taylor argued that there were considerations which made the states' right to reject unconstitutional laws infinitely stronger than that of the federal courts, he did not go on to hold that the state governments were to be regarded as tribunals of last resort in expounding the federal Constitution. In fact, he argued for the doctrine that the central and state governments possessed the right to veto the acts of each other,[84] a doctrine which was later to be adopted and elaborated upon by John C. Calhoun.[85] By the operation of the mutual veto each government would protect the powers that belonged to it against encroachments. Both for Taylor and for Calhoun the mutual veto was part of a larger theory based upon the propositions that power could be checked only by power and that unchecked power inevitably tended toward abuse. The way to preserve liberty in any governmental system was to distribute the governmental powers among various parts of that system, granting to each of these parts the checks necessary to prevent encroachments by the other parts. Because of the nature of power, its distribution without the mutual checks necessary to preserve it was insufficient. Taylor wrote:

[83] *Tyranny Unmasked*, p. 262.   [84] *Ibid.*, pp. 258 ff.
[85] See *infra*, Chap. 5, pp. 142 ff.

If we should even admit, with Mr. Madison, that the government is semi-federal, and semi-national, the question arises, by what means can it be kept so? These are ascertained by the means necessary to maintain a government semi-republican and semi-monarchical. Each moity must counterpoise and check the other. If one principle possesses a supremacy over the other principle, and can remove out of its way all the obstacles which the balancing principle may place in it, the consequences are inevitable; because power can only be checked by power. Therefore an equal capacity in each moity to maintain a government half federal and half national, is as indispensable, as in the case of a government half republican and half monarchical. If the state governments individually, or a bare majority of the states, were supreme, or had a negative over the acts of the federal government, that moity would soon perish, and in like manner, if the federal government should acquire the same power over the state governments, they must perish; just as a limited monarchy would perish if one of its principles obtains a supremacy over the other.[86]

That some collisions between the central and state governments might occur was not a matter of concern to Taylor. Collisions, according to him, served to guarantee that in the final decisions the common interests as opposed to the interests of a particular faction would prevail. His recommendation for the settlement of serious controversies between the central and state governments, should such controversies occur, was an appeal to the people. The control of the people over the governments, and not a dictatorial supremacy of one, or of some portion of one, he declared, acted as an "umpire."[87] Presumably he regarded the people as exercising the control by which the controversies were to be settled when they participated in elections.

Conclusion

The arguments over federalism during the period of Jeffersonian democracy were concerned primarily with the issue of

[86] *New Views of the Constitution*, p. 62.   [87] *Ibid.*, p. 81.

how jurisdictional disputes between the central and state governments of the American union were to be settled. Underlying the Judiciary Act passed by Congress in 1789 and decisions of the United States Supreme Court during the first quarter of the nineteenth century was the assumption that final settlement of such disputes was to be achieved in the regular process of litigation in the federal courts. The courts' decisions would be binding on the respective governments, regardless of who were the immediate parties to the cases litigated. Beginning with the adoption of the Virginia and Kentucky Resolutions of 1798, however, this view concerning the manner in which the political system was to operate was almost constantly under attack. The opposition argument rested in part on the assumption that a perfect legal dualism existed between the central and state governments and in part on assumptions having to do with the nature of compacts, particularly compacts to create federal governments. The central government was not labeled federal in the Virginia and Kentucky Resolutions, the position taken by the authors of these Resolutions being simply that the parties to any compact must interpret for themselves that compact's provisions unless some other authorized interpreter existed. But in the quarter of a century immediately following the adoption of these Resolutions almost constant efforts were made to convey the impression that the central government was a federal as contradistinguished from a national government and that compacts to create federal governments always left the parties to them without a final judge over themselves, a position for which support could be found in the writings of Vattel and Pufendorf.

The importance of semantics could perhaps never be better illustrated than by contrasting the theory of federalism of the Jeffersonian period with that of the period of the framing and adoption of the Constitution. In the earlier of the two periods, it was commonly assumed that a federal system of government must conform to the basic pattern of the system under the existing Articles of Confederation, an assumption which gave the opponents of strong union some of their most potent ammunition to use against adoption of the Constitution. The system provided for by the Constitution was labeled nonfederal by those opposing the Constitution's adoption on the ground that it represented a clear departure from the pattern laid down by the Articles. Now, however, there was a strong desire on the part of those opposing centralized authority to bring this system within the category of federal systems, a desire that was fulfilled by treating a compact among states to create a common government as the only clearly distinguishing feature of a federal system. In other words, the manner in which states entered into the composition of the central authority and the question of whether the central authority was or was not to have direct contact with individual persons became wholly irrelevant matters insofar as the federal or nonfederal character of the system was concerned.

Those who opposed the Constitution during the ratification controversy took the position that it would not, if adopted, be a compact among states but a document to which individual citizens would be parties. Such a position could be avoided, however, if one represented a state as identical with individuals under government rather than with government itself. As Madison suggested both at the time of the ratification of the Constitution and in his Legislative Committee Report of 1800, a state had sometimes been defined as a body of citizens under government and could be thought of as ratifying compacts with other states by popular assent. After 1800, there was a strong tendency to follow this line of reasoning, although a distinction between state and government was by no means always made and although some thought of states and people as being parties to the Constitution in separate capacities.

When a state was distinguished from its governmental institutions and identified with the body of the citizens under these institutions, actually a two-fold purpose was served: First, it was possible to claim that the acts by which the Constitution was ratified were acts of sovereign states and that states and only states were therefore to be regarded as legal parties to the document. Second, it was possible to reconcile the notion of ultimate state sovereignty with the notion of a perfect dualism between the central and state governments in the American union.

A logical conclusion to be deduced from the assumption that ultimate sovereignty was in the states and that a perfect dualism existed between the central and state governments was that any action taken by the central government and believed by a state or its government to be unconstitutional should not be permitted to become effective within the borders of that state. Presumably those who insisted that there was a right of state interposition usually intended to support some such conclusion. However, the most important statement that might be made about state interposition during the Jeffersonian era is that it was a phrase which could be used with considerable effectiveness in stirring popular emotions. Although the language in which the phrase was embodied was almost always of an inflamatory character, it was seldom so definite as to prevent those using it from escaping the charge that they advocated a course of action not generally admitted to be in keeping with the provisions of the Constitution. Madison seems to have been alone in elaborating on courses of action which interposition might include, and those which he mentioned were of such a character that no one could dispute their constitutionality. What he said amounted to a watering down of state sovereignty to the extent that it had to mean a sovereignty under law. Perhaps the most important of the courses of action he mentioned was that of constitutional amendment. The role of the states regarding amendments to the Constitution could be taken to imply that the states possessed an authority superior to any authority possessed by the central government. But if the authority to amend the Constitution was to be called sovereignty, it had to be a sovereignty which could be exercised only in accordance with established legal procedures.

[*To avoid monarchy or disunion*] *it is indispensable that the government of the United States should be restored to its federal character. Nothing short of a perfect restoration, as it came from the hands of its framers, can avert them. It is folly to suppose that any popular government, except one strictly federal, in* practice, *as well as in* theory, *can last, over a country of such vast extent and diversity of interests and institutions. It would not be more irrational to suppose, that it could last, without the responsibility of the rulers to the ruled. The tendency of the former to oppress the latter, is not stronger than is the tendency of the more powerful section, to oppress the weaker. Nor is the right of suffrage more indispensable to enforce the responsibility of the rulers to the ruled, than a* federal organization, *to compel the parts to respect the rights of each other. It requires the united action of both to prevent the abuse of power and oppression; and to constitute, really and truly, a constitutional government. To supersede either, is to convert it* in fact, *whatever may be its* theory, *into an absolute government.*

But it cannot be restored to its federal character, without restoring the separate governments of the several states, and the states themselves, to their true position. From the latter the whole system emanated. . . .

—John C. Calhoun, "A Discourse on the Constitution and Government of the United States," in *The Works of John C. Calhoun,* ed. Richard K. Crallé (New York, 1854-57), I, 381-82.

(5)

The Same Subject Continued

CONTROVERSY OVER THE NATURE OF THE AMERICAN union under the Constitution has reached acute stages when the opposing sides have been large geographic sections which are motivated by some immediate interests into taking extreme positions. Such a stage was reached during the presidency of James Madison when the federal embargo legislation and the war against England were supported by most of the country but met with united opposition from the New England states. But the most important of all of the sectional controversies in American history was the one between the North and the South which began in the 1820's and continued almost unabated until after the Civil War. The economic and humanitarian differences between these sections which led to this controversy are well known to students of American history. What is important for our attention here is the strong particularist position which the South came more and more to support as it sought to prevent the enactment and enforcement of protective tariff legislation and also to prevent any interference with the institution of slavery. Although a minority section, it endeavored to maintain a perfect balance between itself and the North in the determination of federal policy. When the devices on which it relied for this purpose failed, it made its decision to secede from the union.

The appeal of the South was above all an appeal to the doctrine of state sovereignty. It was an appeal to the same general theory of union resorted to by particularists of the Jeffersonian era. Now this theory was more extensively elaborated, greater precision being given to some of the legal conceptions employed and more attention being directed to explaining how the American system of government was to function in practice if the premise of complete state sovereignty was granted. For a large number of southern leaders state interposition avowedly became state nullification—not state nullification as an extra-constitutional measure, as Jefferson probably thought of it, but state nullification as a thoroughly constitutional and peaceable means of checking federal "encroachments" on minority rights.

John C. Calhoun

South Carolinians were chiefly responsible for the refinements and extensions of the earlier particularist arguments. Embittered by high import duties levied by Congress in 1828, the State of South Carolina soon became the center of a well-organized states' rights movement which manifested itself in numerous publications and public meetings, and also in formal state action. The legislature of the state solemnly protested against the Tariff Act of 1828, the House of Representatives going on to order the publication of 5,000 copies of a lengthy "Exposition" devoted to the economics of tariff legislation and to the protection of minority rights by state interposition. In 1832 this state became the only state ever to adopt a formal nullification ordinance directed against a federal legislative measure, and in 1860 it became the first state to adopt an ordinance of secession from the union under the United States Constitution.

The most prominent of the South Carolina participants in the states' rights movement was John C. Calhoun, who was prepared for the role he played by superior natural talents, by legal training, and by long experience in public office. His public service began in 1808 and ran almost continuously until his death in 1850. It included 22 years as a member of Congress, first as representative and then as senator from South Carolina, nearly eight years as secretary of war (1817-1825), seven years as vice-president of the United States (1825-1832), and one year as United States secretary of state (1844-1845). During the first part of this long career, Calhoun's outlook was generally nationalistic, as is illustrated by his support of the central government's program for internal improvements and by his support of protective import duties levied by Congress in 1816. By 1828, however, this outlook was very definitely changed. Calhoun secretly authored the South Carolina "Exposition" of 1828, and within five years of this date was the undisputed intellectual leader of southern sectionalism.

Calhoun both demonstrated remarkable skill in the handling of abstract legal conceptions and contributed to the philosophy of minority protection with his general theory of a concurrent majority. This theory may be regarded as supplying his moral justification for what he claimed as a legal right. In his *Disquisition on Government*, the work in which the theory of a concurrent majority is most elaborately set forth, he first made the common assumption that government, while necessary to prevent self-seeking individuals from overreaching and exploiting their fellows, needs to be checked in order to prevent the abuse of power. He explained that the powers it needs to preserve order must be administered by men, in whom the individual feelings are stronger than the social.[1] But he went on to argue that the control which was necessary to hold government to its proper function and to prevent it from engaging in wrongful actions was not supplied by popular suffrage. Popular suffrage, he reasoned, would be an adequate check on rulers only if all members of the community had the same interests. But this sort of situation did not exist anywhere. One of the most obvious facts in human history, Calhoun assumed, was the existence in any community of a variety of interest groups, each desiring to obtain possession of the powers of government. If a single interest group were not strong enough to attain the objective, combinations of groups whose interests

[1] Calhoun, *The Works of John C. Calhoun*, ed. R. K. Crallé, I, 7.

were similar would be formed. Thus in time parties arose, and eventually a whole community was divided between two great parties, one in possession of the government and enjoying the advantages of this possession, the other seeking to obtain the possession and along with it the advantages. The majority, through the suffrage, was indeed able to hold the officers of the government accountable to itself, but the suffrage by itself afforded no protection to the minority. The majority, whose members constituted in fact the real rulers, was in a position constantly to aggrandize itself at the expense of the rest of the community. Moreover, since it was made up of men in whom the individual feelings were stronger than the social, it would show the same tendency to abuse power to be expected of any ruler not subject to popular election. In order to give protection to the whole community against the abuse of governmental powers, some device, in addition to popular suffrage, was therefore necessary.[2]

The device that would give the desired protection was the concurrent majority. This majority differed from a numerical majority in that it collected the sense not of the greater number of citizens but of the interests within the political community. It might indeed be difficult, if not impossible, to organize the government in such a way as to give full representation to every interest; but the desired end would be largely if not fully achieved if the sense of a few and prominent interests was collected. If this were done, "it would require so large a portion of the community, compared with the whole, to concur, or acquiesce in the action of the government, that the number to be plundered would be too few, and the number to be aggrandized too many, to afford adequate motives to oppression and the abuse of its powers."[3]

Calhoun argued that the concurrent majority principle would, where adopted, produce a spirit of harmony and compromise, in contrast to the party or factional strife that pre-

[2] *Ibid.*, I, 13 ff.   [3] *Ibid.*, I, 24-27.

vailed in communities whose governments were based on the principle of rule by simple numerical majorities. Where each interest of a community had the power of self-protection, all strife between the various interests for ascendancy was prevented; for each interest group saw that it could best promote its own prosperity by displaying a conciliatory attitude and by promoting the prosperity of the other interest groups within the community. Instead of faction and struggle for party ascendancy, there was "patriotism, nationality, harmony, and a struggle only for supremacy in promoting the common good of the whole."[4] There was no cause to fear that it would be difficult under the principle of the concurrent majority to bring the various conflicting interests of the community to unite on a policy, for the necessity of the case and an ardent patriotism would lead to compromise.

> Impelled by the imperious necessity of preventing the suspension of the action of government, with the fatal consequences to which it would lead, and by the strong additional impulse derived from an ardent love of country, each portion would regard the sacrifice it would have to make by yielding its peculiar interest to secure the common interest and safety of all, including its own, as nothing compared to the evils that would be inflicted on all, including its own, by pertinaciously adhering to a different line of action.[5]

Calhoun appears usually to have associated the concurrent majority principle not with state sovereignty as he defined it but simply with the role which states as corporate entities had in the composition of the central government.[6] For example, it is clear from his *Discourse on the Constitution and Government of the United States* that he thought of the equal representation of states in the United States Senate as affording one of the best examples of the incorporation of the principle in the central government. The principle operated success-

[4] *Ibid.*, I, 48-49.   [5] *Ibid.*, I, 68.
[6] *Ibid.*, I, 168 ff.

fully when a minority of the voting population controlled
enough states, and thus enough votes in the Senate, to defeat a
measure desired and initiated by a numerical majority in control of the House of Representatives or one or more of the
other branches of government. However, the principle was
broad enough in meaning to include nullification by a state or
by its government of a measure which had been formally
adopted by the central government; in fact, Calhoun eventually came to the conclusion that this check was an indispensable means of affording protection to the minority below the
Mason and Dixon Line. In analyzing the political alignments of
the second quarter of the nineteenth century, he saw a party
combination concentrated in the northern section of the country which not only included a majority of the electorate but
also a majority of the states. Since it possessed both majorities,
this combination was in a position to control indefinitely the
three departments of the central government and thus to bring
about the adoption by that government of any measures it
chose no matter how the measures might affect southern interests.[7]

In defending the right of a state or its government to nullify
a measure of the central government, Calhoun adopted a definition of the term "federal" that was slightly unlike any definition of the term that had previously been advanced. The
term was still to be associated with the idea of state sovereignty, but it was inapplicable to most of the political systems
which had been created in the past by the union of pre-existing states. Calhoun declared the central government of the
United States to be a federal government in contradistinction
to a national government on the one hand and to a confederacy
on the other. It was federal and not national because it was a
government of states united in a political union, not a government of individuals socially united by what was usually called
a social compact.[8] For proof that it was a government of states

[7] *Ibid.*, I, 223 ff.   [8] *Ibid.*, I, 112-13.

united in a political union, Calhoun reviewed in detail the historical evidence relating to the independence of the thirteen British American colonies and the formation of the American union. He insisted that the colonies had acted as separate and distinct communities in declaring independence, pointing out that the Declaration of Independence was made by delegates appointed by the several colonies and that the delegation of each colony had cast a single vote in approving the Declaration. These communities had been declared in the Declaration and in the later Articles of Confederation to be free and independent states, and they had acted as distinct and sovereign communities in ordaining and establishing the United States Constitution. State-appointed delegates, who voted by states and whose votes were counted by states, had constituted the Convention that framed the Constitution. After its framing, the Constitution had been ratified by each state, and it was binding on a state only in consequence of its being ratified by that state. That the framers had understood the government which they were establishing to be a federal and not a national government was to be inferred from the language which they had used. In his letter submitting the Constitution to the Congress of the existing Confederation, General Washington, the president of the Convention, had referred to the proposed new government as " 'the general government of the Union' " and as the " 'federal government of these states.' " Some members of the Convention had indeed favored a national government, and in their plans the constitution and government had been styled national. But those favoring a federal government had finally gained the ascendancy, and the term "national" was replaced by the term "United States." To the delegates in the Convention the expressions " 'the federal government of the United States,' " " 'the general government of the Union,' " and " 'government of the United States,' " had all meant the same thing, i.e., a federal, not a national government.[9] Examin-

[9] *Ibid.*, I, 113 ff.

ing the usage of these expressions in the Revolutionary period
and under the Articles of Confederation, Calhoun reached the
conclusion that the framers, in drafting the Constitution, had
meant to leave the states in substantially the same relation to
each other as had existed during the Revolutionary period and
under the Articles of Confederation.[10]

What was one to do with the statement in the Preamble of
the Constitution in which the people of the United States declare that they are ordaining and establishing the Constitution?
Calhoun took the term "people" in this statement to mean the
peoples of the several states and not the people of the union
taken in the aggregate. He observed that the framers had omit-
ted an enumeration of the states by name after the word
"people" because it had been impossible to ascertain which
states would become members of the new union. He called
attention to the fact that the first draft of the Constitution had
contained this enumeration and that it had been dropped after
the adoption of the Constitution's Seventh Article providing
that the ratifications of nine states would be sufficient to
establish the Constitution between those nine.[11]

Calhoun went on to emphasize the role of the states in the
composition of the central government, taking the position
that every division of that government directly or indirectly
represented states in their corporate capacities.[12] He called
attention to the fact that the members of the United States
Senate were elected by the legislatures of the states, and argued that the members of the House of Representatives were
elected by the people of the states not as composing mere
districts of one great community but as composing distinct
and independent communities. He pointed out that the president and vice-president were chosen by electors appointed by
their respective states. He also held that appointments to fed-

[10] *Ibid.*, I, 116.   [11] *Ibid.*, I, 128-29, 133.   [12] *Ibid.*, I, 137.

eral judgeships were state appointments, since the president
and senators who made these appointments owed their own
offices to the states.[13]

Further proof that the central government was a government of states and was therefore federal could be found in the
Fifth Article of the Constitution, which provided for this
instrument's amendment by both the affirmative action of
two-thirds of both houses of Congress or of a specially called
convention and the separate affirmative action of three-fourths
of the states or of three-fourths of their legislatures. According to Calhoun, this Article showed conclusively that the people of the several states still retained "that supreme ultimate
power, called sovereignty;—the power by which they ordained and established the Constitution; and which can right-
fully create, modify, amend, or abolish it, at its pleasure."[14]
The states had indeed departed from the principle of unanimous consent in the provisions for amendments to the Constitution; they had "agreed, for their mutual convenience and
advantage, to modify, by compact, their high sovereign power
of creating and establishing constitutions, as far as it related to
the Constitution and government of the United States." But
that the states did not intend to divest themselves of the high
sovereign right to change or abolish that Constitution and government at their pleasure was not to be doubted. That sovereigns might by compact modify or qualify the exercise of
their power without impairing their sovereignty was, Calhoun
claimed, an acknowledged principle. It was a principle that
was strikingly illustrated by the confederacy that existed at
the time the Constitution was formed.[15]

This at least seems to mean unqualified acceptance of
Vattel's dictum that states might by compact unite to create a
federal system without themselves ceasing to be perfect states.
In his speech in the United States Senate of February 26, 1833,

[13] Ibid., I, 137-38.   [14] Ibid., I, 138.
[15] Ibid., I, 139.

Calhoun quoted from the appendix of Tucker's *Blackstone* a long passage in which the dictum appears, without, however, indicating any awareness that the dictum was to be traced to the famous Swiss publicist. In quoting the passage, Calhoun meant to be invoking the authority of Burlamaqui, another writer relied upon by Tucker.[16]

Remaining consistently logical, Calhoun ruled out the not uncommon assumption that the Constitution was to be regarded as national in reference to the powers that had been delegated to the central government and as federal in reference to the powers that had been reserved to the states. In this connection he emphasized that the term "federal" implied a league which in turn implied a compact among sovereign communities. It was true that the idea of a federal constitution and government also implied both power delegated by mutual agreement to a common council or government and power reserved to states, but the federal character of the system was not to be deduced simply from the fact that certain powers were reserved to the states. This deduction would have to be based on the absurd assumption that the constitution was federal in reference to a class of powers which were expressly excluded from it. Moreover, when the nature of delegated powers was properly understood it would be clear that the delegation of powers to the central government had in no sense had the effect of consolidating the people of the states into a single nation. Under the American system of government all powers were trust powers. Thus the powers delegated to the central government had been granted in trust and not absolutely transferred to this government.[17]

If the delegated powers were considered as having been absolutely surrendered, inexplicable difficulties would present themselves. There was first the perplexing question of how the people of the states could be partly sovereign and partly not sovereign, sovereign as to the reserved and not sovereign as to the delegated powers. Calhoun wrote:

> There is no difficulty in understanding how powers appertaining to sovereignty, may be divided; and *the exercise* of one portion delegated to one set of agents, and another portion to another: or how sovereignty may be vested in one man, or in a few, or in many. But how sovereignty itself—the supreme power—can be divided,—how the people of the several states can be partly sovereign and partly *not* sovereign—partly supreme, and partly *not* supreme, it is impossible to conceive. Sovereignty is an entire thing;—to divide, is,—to destroy it.[18]

If, when the United States Constitution was adopted, it had been possible to divide sovereignty and thus to transfer absolutely the powers delegated or granted, a difficulty would have arisen from the lack of a recipient for the sovereignty surrendered by the states. The central government could not have been a recipient, for this would have subverted the fundamental principle that sovereignty resides in the people. For sovereignty to have been transferred at all it would have to have been transferred to the people considered in the aggregate as a nation. But that such transfer actually occurred was opposed not only by a force of reason which could not be resisted but also by the Preamble and by the declaration in the Tenth Amendment to the Constitution stating that the powers that were not delegated to the United States were reserved to the states or to the people.[19]

There were those, according to Calhoun, who admitted the Constitution to be wholly federal and who yet insisted that the government provided for by it was partly federal and partly national.[20] The origin of this theory he attributed to the authors of the *Federalist*, quoting from Madison's comments in Numbers 39 and 40. Madison had not actually referred to the

---

[18] *Ibid.*, I, 146.   [19] *Ibid.*, I, 146.
[20] *Ibid.*, I, 150.

Constitution as exclusively federal, but he had argued that it was to be a compact among states and had gone on to describe the government for which it provided as partly federal and partly national. Calhoun's complaint against Madison's analysis of the proposed new system was really that Madison had assumed the legal character of the system to be determined as much by the arrangement of the system's superstructure as by the foundation on which it rested. Calhoun insisted that the Constitution determined the character of the central government, that it was impossible to conceive of the Constitution as wholly federal and this government as partly federal and partly national. He was unimpressed by Madison's interpretation of the provisions of the Constitution allotting representation in the United States House of Representatives in proportion to the states' respective populations, and allotting presidential and vice-presidential electors among the states partially on this same basis. According to Madison, these provisions implied that the legislative and executive branches derived their powers partially from the people considered in the aggregate as forming one nation; but Calhoun did not agree that this idea was implicit. Against this assumption he advanced, as a fundamental and universally admitted principle, the proposition that all the powers of the government were derived from the Constitution, and reiterated his argument that both the members of the House of Representatives and the presidential and vice-presidential electors represented the states as sovereign members of the union.[21] Nor did Calhoun agree with Madison's assumption that the departure from the principle of unanimous consent by the states for amending the Constitution had made the amending power partly national. In opposing this assumption, he argued that the amending power was derived from the states in their original, distinct, and sovereign character. The amending power, he insisted, was but a modification of the original creating power by which the Constitution

[21] *Ibid.*, I, 153 ff.

THE SAME SUBJECT CONTINUED

was ordained and established; it was not a negation or inhibition of that power.[22]

How, then, was the political system under the Constitution to be distinguished from a confederacy? In answering this question Calhoun found points both of difference and of agreement between the system and a confederacy and between the system and a national government. It differed from a national government and was similar to a confederacy in having for its basis a confederacy and not a nation, but it differed from a confederacy and agreed with a national government in being in fact a government and not a mere congress of delegates. In a confederacy the congress or "council" was more nearly allied to an assembly of diplomats convened to deliberate and determine how a league or treaty between their several sovereigns should be carried into execution, the members being left to furnish their quota of means and to co-operate in carrying out the decisions of the congress or council. A federal government, however, was to the extent of the powers delegated to it as much a government as a national government, even though it was based upon a confederacy.[23]

The substitution of a government for the Congress of the Confederation was, according to Calhoun, the "great and essential change" that had been made by the Constitutional Convention of 1787. But he went on to explain that this change had involved other significant changes. It had been necessary to transfer the source of delegated powers from the governments of the states to the people of the states. The governments of the states had ratified the Articles of Confederation, but only the sovereign people of the states were competent to form a constitution and government. The political association that had been ordained and established by the people in their character of sovereign and independent communities was in truth a union, which could not have been made more intimate without destroying the states. On the other hand, the confederacy under the Articles had been a league of the governments of states, or of states through the agency of their governments. Under the Articles it had been unnecessary to have a careful enumeration of the delegated powers, since the Confederation Congress had to depend upon the co-operation of the states for carrying into execution the powers it exercised. But under the Constitution a careful enumeration of the delegated powers had been necessary in order to avoid a collision between these powers and the powers reserved to the states. Under the Articles the relation of the governments of the states to the body which represented them in their confederated character was the relation of superior to subordinate, of creator to creature. But the relation between the state and central governments under the Constitution was a relation of equals and co-ordinates, because both state and central governments derived their powers from, and were ordained and established by, the same authority, namely, the people of the several states. As a government the central authority under the Constitution had necessarily been given both the right to decide in the first instance on the extent of its powers, and, unlike the Congress of the Confederation, the right to act directly upon individuals in carrying its powers into execution.[24]

While Calhoun conceded that the central government under the Constitution had the right to determine the extent of its powers in the first instance, he by no means intended to concede that this government had the right to make its judgment final and binding on all when the judgment was opposed by one or more of the governments of the states. On this point he sharply distinguished between a government with full possession of all of the powers appertaining to government and a government within a system of co-ordinate governments. He explained that the former had the right to enforce its judgment regarding the extent of its powers against all opposition but that a similar right could not be allowed to one of the gov-

[24] *Ibid.*, I, 164 ff.

ernments within the latter without also allowing the right to each of the governments in the system. To allow the right to each of the governments he deemed untenable, since this would leave the umpirage to brute force when there was conflict between the governments over the extent of their respective powers.[25]

Calhoun repeatedly made the assumption that a legal division of powers between two governments left to the final interpretation of one of the governments was no legal division at all. He explained that in such a case one of the governments held powers as a mere tenant at will and that it would be deprived of its portion at such time as the other chose to assume the whole.[26] Nor would it, according to him, make any significant difference if final decisions regarding the division were left to the judiciary of one of the governments. Thus the notion that the federal courts of the United States were satisfactory organs to render final decisions on the jurisdictional boundary between the central and state governments was to be rejected. The "independent tenure" of the federal judges might indeed be of some effectiveness in shielding them from political influence, but it was no guarantee that they would be impartial in deciding cases dealing with the extent of the central government's powers. Therefore it afforded no real protection against federal encroachments on the reserved powers of the states. Complete impartiality was not to be expected of judges who had hopes of obtaining higher office and were subject to impeachment. The associate justices of the Supreme Court were to be expected to aspire to the office of chief justice, and they, as well as the chief justice were to be expected to aspire to the highest post of the central government. Thus, the judges would lean toward the side which could control popular elections and which, through elections, could control patronage. If the independence of the judiciary were not compromised by the judges' desire for advancement or their fear

[25] *Ibid.*, I, 241-43.   [26] *Ibid.*, I, 243.

of impeachment, there was always the possibility of influencing the judiciary when new judges were appointed. In time, Calhoun declared, the bench would be filled with those whose opinions accorded with the other departments. He predicted that the judiciary would ultimately yield to the control of the numerically dominant section of the union.[27]

From his assumption that the central and state governments were perfect co-ordinates, Calhoun went on to adopt the idea of the mutual negative which previously had been advanced by John Taylor. That is, the central and state governments had the right to veto the acts of each other. The operation of this mutual negative afforded to each of the governments a means of protecting the powers which had been allotted to it.[28] Its effect was supposed to be to arrest the exercise of a disputed power until such time as the Constitution could be amended to declare the power actually possessed by the government which had sought to exercise it. In the South Carolina "Exposition" of 1828, Calhoun noted that Section 25 of the federal Judiciary Act of 1789 had, in authorizing appeals from state courts to the United States Supreme Court, in effect conferred on the Supreme Court the right to nullify state measures whenever in the Court's opinion such measures conflicted with powers delegated to the central government. This, he observed, afforded complete protection to the central government against encroachments by the governments of the states. What he complained of was a prevalent failure to recognize that there was in the states a corresponding right to nullify measures of the central government. Because of a misconception of the nature of the American system of government and of the nature of government in general, the Supreme Court was being relied on not only to protect the central government from encroachments of the state governments but also to protect the state governments from encroachments of the central government.[29]

[27] *Ibid.*, I, 337-38.   [28] *Ibid.*, I, 244.
[29] *Ibid.*, VI, 38 ff.

Under the operation of the mutual negative, how could the central and state governments avoid conflict and a serious disruption of the union? In the *Discourse* Calhoun anticipated this question and proceeded to give an answer to it. First, he pointed out that collision and conflict were incident to every division of powers. They were evils that were incident to all constitutional government, and the choice between constitutional government and absolute government lay between the evil and good incident to each. For the United States the choice lay between two governments—the one a national, consolidated, and irresponsible government of a dominant section of the country and the other a federal, constitutional, and responsible government with all the division of powers necessary to form and preserve such a government in a vast country with great diversity of interests and institutions.[30] But Calhoun professed to believe that the mutual negative, far from contributing to collision and conflict between the central and state governments, would, if put into practice, have just the opposite effect. It was from encroachments by one of the co-ordinate governments on the domain of another that much of the collision and conflict in the American union actually sprang, and the aim and end of the mutual negative was to prevent such encroachments.[31]

Calhoun also anticipated that the mutual negative would be objected to on the ground that it left the way open for the numerous state governments to hamper the central government in performing its legitimate functions. This objection he conceded to be plausible, but he insisted that the negative to be exercised by the state governments was not a stronger check than was actually required to keep the central government within its proper sphere. He maintained that it was a weaker negative than that exercised by the Roman tribunate, which negative he claimed had proven to be no stronger than was necessary to resist the positive power of the government of

[30] *Ibid.*, I, 268.   [31] *Ibid.*, I, 269.

Rome. Unlike the negative of the Roman tribunes, which extended to all the acts of government, the negative to be exercised by the state governments extended only to the execution of such acts of the central government as might present a question involving the division of powers between this government and the governments of the states. Established to protect the plebeians from oppression and abuse of power on the part of the Roman Senate, the Roman tribunes had ordinarily been disposed to exercise their negative. However, in the habitual relationship between state and central governments of the United States, the power and interests of the majority of the state governments identified with the power and interests of the central government and thus disposed this majority to enlarge and sustain the central government rather than resist its encroachments. As viewed by this majority, their powers were extended rather than contracted by the encroachments. Only a minority of the state governments would be disposed to exercise a negative on federal actions. Experience had proven that even that minority would have within its own limits another large minority which would be opposed to it and would be identified in views and party feelings with the majority in control of the central government. Moreover, hoping in their turn to gain the ascendancy, the majority in the states opposing federal encroachments would be adverse to taking a stand against such encroachments. This majority would naturally be disinclined to weaken its party connections with the minority in the other states whose interest and feelings, aside from party ties, would be with the majority of those states. Finally, it was to be remembered that the federal Constitution provided that all the functionaries of the state governments, as well as all those of the central government, should be bound by oath or affirmation to support the Constitution, and that the decision of the highest tribunal should be final as between the parties to a case in controversy.[32]

Calhoun did not reach the conclusion that the negative of

[32] *Ibid.*, I, 269 ff.

the state governments would never hamper the central government in the performance of its legitimate functions, but he did argue that the forces militating against use of the negative would be so formidable as almost to eliminate any danger that it would result in any serious derangement or disorder. Such danger, he in effect insisted, would be nothing when compared to the danger that the state governments would be too disposed to acquiesce in federal encroachments.[33]

Aside from the mutual negative which was to operate between the central and state governments, there was also a negative which might be exercised by a state in its high sovereign capacity as a party to the constitutional compact by which the union had been created. As a party to this compact, a state had the right to determine the extent of the obligations which the compact imposed. The principle on which this rested, Calhoun argued, was essential to the nature of compacts and was in accord with universal practice. The right of states to determine the extent of the obligations imposed by the constitutional compact necessarily involved two additional rights: pronouncing a federal act in conformity or not in conformity with the compact's provisions and pronouncing an act judged inconsistent with these provisions to be null, void, and of no effect. Determining for themselves the mode and measure of redress to be adopted, the states could interpose for the purpose of arresting within their respective limits an act which they had found to be void. By the exercise of this right of interposition the delegated powers were prevented from encroaching on the reserved powers.[34]

Calhoun conceded that the right of state interposition must be exercised with caution and with due regard to a state's obligations as a member of the union. The more important a right was and the more delicate its character the higher was the obligation to observe strictly the rules of prudence and propriety in exercising it. The right of state interposition,

which Calhoun called the most important and delicate by far
of all the rights appertaining to the people of the several states
as members of a common union, should, he warned, be exercised with the greatest caution and forbearance. It should be
exercised only when, in the opinion of the states exercising it,
there had been a clear and palpable infraction of the constitutional compact. Even then the states were bound to forbear
interposition unless the infraction was highly dangerous in its
character and appeared to admit of no other remedy. If interposition were employed, it should be undertaken in good faith,
not to weaken or to destroy the union but to uphold and preserve it by causing the instrument on which it rested to be observed and respected. The mode and measure of redress employed by a state should be limited exclusively to procedures
necessary to preserve the union.[35]

Calhoun did not go so far as to assume that the states' sense
of moral obligation would itself be sufficient to prevent them
from abusing the right of interposition. Prudence and propriety were by themselves insufficient to prevent abuse of the
right, he observed, and this would have to be conceded by
anyone who was in the least acquainted with that constitution
of man's nature which made governments necessary. By themselves the highest moral obligations offered but feeble resistance to the abuse of power; but in the American union these
obligations were supplemented by many powerful influences
of a less elevated character which were well calculated to prevent abuse of the high and delicate right of state interposition.
These influences, as explained by Calhoun, were largely identical with those restraining state governments in the exercise of
their negative on federal actions. Just as the majority of the
state governments would be disposed to enlarge and sustain
central authority rather than resist its encroachments, so also
would a majority of the states and their populations, estimated
in federal numbers, support the central government when

[35] *Ibid.*, I, 279-80.

questions arose between it and a state involving an infraction of the Constitution. There was also the strength of the party ties of two great political parties extending over the union, the resistance which a minority party in a state would offer to threatened interposition by that state, and the reluctance of the leaders of the majority in a state to take a stand which would render them both odious to the majority of the union and unpopular with their own party in other states.[36]

A final safeguard was to be found, according to Calhoun, in the authority which amended the Constitution. It was this authority which, in a case involving disputed jurisdiction, could declare with certainty what the Constitution meant. When the central government claimed a power which was contested by a state, it was incumbent upon the central government to seek to make good its claim by an appeal to the amending authority. This duty to invoke the amending authority was viewed by Calhoun as based on the "clear and well established principle" that a party claiming a power was bound to make good its claim by appealing to higher authority when such authority had been provided.[37]

Calhoun anticipated the possible suggestion that a state or a state's government might forbear the exercise of its negative and itself appeal to the amending authority. But this procedure for determining whether the central government possessed the power which it claimed was, he insisted, wholly unsatisfactory and, in fact, impossible of application. He pointed out that the procedure would leave the central government in full possession of the contested power while the state sought to invoke the amending authority. In addition, he argued that an appeal to the amending authority was not open to a state as it was open to the central government. Backed by the majority which had brought about the enactment of the contested measure, the central government could appeal to the amending power at pleasure. On the other hand, the state, which

---

[36] *Ibid.*, I, 281 ff.   [37] *Ibid.*, I, 284, 295-97.

would be of the minority opposing the measure, could not possibly muster the support necessary to set the amending authority in motion.[38] A state negative, or a negative by a state government, was the real way to set it in motion. This had the effect of suspending the central government's exercise of a disputed power and thus of forcing that government to resort to the amending authority. On the other hand, if the disputed power were allowed to be fully exercised while a state sought to appeal to this authority, the central government would have every motive to prevent the amending authority from being successful and to defeat action on the appeal.[39]

A disagreement between the central government and a state government over their respective jurisdictions was regarded by Calhoun as finally settled when a decision was reached through the amending process. If the decision went against the central government, that government should abandon the power it had sought to exercise. If the decision supported the central government, the negative of the state government was overruled, and the disputed act became operative within the limits of the state.[40] A case involving the interposition of a state in its sovereign character was in a somewhat different category. Here the state was bound to acquiesce in the decision reached by the amending process if the act of the central government was consistent with the character of the Constitution and the ends for which it was established and was thus fairly within the scope of the amending authority. If it was not, the state was not bound to acquiesce in the decision. In such a case it could choose to secede from the union. It made known its election to stay in the union by rescinding the act by which it had interposed its authority and bound its citizens to disobedience to the federal act in question. A failure to rescind was itself tantamount to secession.[41]

Aside from defending the ultimate right of state secession, Calhoun's argument was in sum an argument alleging that

[38] *Ibid.*, I, 297-98.   [39] *Ibid.*, I, 298-99.
[40] *Ibid.*, I, 299-300.   [41] *Ibid.*, I, 300-01.

the function of umpiring the American federal system belonged exclusively to the authority which amended the Constitution and not to the federal judiciary. Of course, he was on firm ground in representing a constitutional amendment as superior to any prior decision of courts of law or any governmental functionaries. Also favoring his position was the lack of any provision in the Constitution which could be said to remove all doubt that the role of umpiring the federal system had been delegated to the federal courts. But as was noted in Chapter 3, the debates over the ratification of the Constitution do contain evidence that some of the participants assumed that adjudication either in federal courts alone or in federal and state courts would settle controversies over the jurisdictional boundaries of the central and state governments.[42] There is no evidence to the effect that any of those who framed and adopted the Constitution intended that a state or a state's government should be able to force an appeal to the amending authority for a declaration of the meaning of the Constitution. Calhoun's claim that this right existed had to rest solely on the unproven assumption that the states were ultimately sovereign and that the central and state governments were perfect legal equals.

Aside from the constitutional question of the right of a state or a state's government to nullify a measure of the central government, there were, of course, the practical difficulties which the exercise of the right must involve. The really astonishing part of Calhoun's argument was his contention that the American federal system might be expected to function with a high degree of harmony and with sufficient energy at the center if the states and their governments were allowed to possess the negatives which he claimed for them. It was one thing to insist upon full protection for all large interest groups even at the price of a serious disruption of the union. It was quite another thing to insist that it was pos-

[42] See *supra*, pp. 86-87.

sible to have this protection and a durable and effective union at the same time. Calhoun was insisting that it was possible to have both. But aside from the prospect that the central government would confine itself within the strictest limits, there was nothing to guarantee harmony. Of course, the central government, because of the likelihood of having its will immediately thwarted, might decide not to attempt the exercise of powers which it believed itself to possess. On the other hand, if it went ahead and exercised such powers as it believed it had and desired to exercise, there was really no reason to hope that negatives would not be used, although Calhoun argued otherwise. Some persons in every state would be opposed to resorting to the negatives. But it is pertinent at this point to note that throughout the history of federal systems the members have not hesitated to exercise whatever rights they believe themselves to possess. Moreover, it could be argued that the weight which Calhoun gave to factors which might be expected to incline states and their governments against unwarranted or excessive use of the negatives was inconsistent with his earlier argument regarding the intensity of partisan strife and the tendency of political parties in the United States to become more and more sectional.

While the authority which amended the Constitution might eventually resolve a conflict, years might pass before it did so. Thus, if the negatives for which Calhoun contended were permitted, it was almost unthinkable that the federal system would function as a single entity with a unified body of law. Since a negative by a state or by its government was to effect an arrest in executing a measure of the central government within the borders of that state while having no effect on its execution in other states, the law of the land might vary constantly from one part of the country to another.

The practical difficulties involved in the doctrine of nullification were pointed out by the aged Madison. Whatever might have been his views during the controversy over the Alien and Sedition Acts of 1798, in 1830 and in succeeding years he reaffirmed in unmistakable terms the position he had taken in the *Federalist*. That is to say, he held that the United States Supreme Court was the tribunal of last resort to decide controversies relating to the jurisdictional boundary between the central and state governments. A state might seek to have a decision of the Court reversed by constitutional amendment, but it had no constitutional right to force an appeal to the amending authority by nullifying a federal measure. It was obvious, said Madison, that a right in each state to decide for itself the jurisdictional boundary could not fail to make the Constitution and laws of the United States different in different states. Nor was it less obvious that a diversity of independent decisions would altogether distract the government of the union and speedily put an end to the union itself. A uniform authority of the laws was itself a vital principle.[43]

Other Southern Protagonists

We will not attempt to analyze here the writings of the numerous other South Carolina authors of this period who dealt with the nature of the American union. Many of them simply reasserted the doctrines propounded by Calhoun.[44] However, some of the particularist arguments advanced during this period in other southern states are of interest.

There was no marked tendency among southern leaders outside of South Carolina during the pre-Civil War years to support nullification as a constitutional and peaceable means

---

[43] See *Letters and Other Writings of James Madison*, 4 vols. (Philadelphia, 1865), IV, 96-101, 196, 205-06, 296-97, 410. A recent criticism of the doctrine of nullification in which the practical difficulties it involves are emphasized is included in an essay by Louis Hartz entitled "South Carolina vs. the United States," in *America in Crisis*, ed. Daniel Aaron (New York, 1952), pp. 73-89.

[44] For examples, see the following pamphlets: Thomas Cooper, *Consolidation*, 2nd ed. (Columbia, S.C., 1830); [Maria Pinckney], *The Quintessence of Long Speeches* (Charleston, S.C., 1830); William Harper, *Speech before the Charleston State Rights and Free Trade Association*, April 1, 1832 (Charleston, S.C., 1832); and William Harper, *The Remedy of State Interposition or Nullification* (Charleston, S.C., 1832).

of redressing measures of the central government. In fact, it seems not improbable that many southern leaders of this period were fearful lest the doctrine of nullification prove to be a boomerang. It might possibly result in vetoes by northern states of federal measures already on the statute books which favored southern rather than northern interests. In any event, there is some evidence of concern in the South over the prospect that northern states might refuse to respect their obligation under existing federal law to return to their southern owners fugitive slaves who sought haven in the North.[45] Nevertheless, there was in the three decades which immediately preceded the Civil War no lack of emphasis outside of South Carolina on the notions that the states of the American union were sovereign, that a sovereign state was to be recognized as having complete control over its own destiny come what may, and that coercion of the members of a federal system was never justifiable. Presumably the right of one of the American states to control its own destiny was always understood to include a right to withdraw from the union. What it meant short of this was usually not made clear.

Three prominent southerners who both reflected and helped to mould southern opinion in this same period were George M. Troup, of Georgia, and Abel P. Upshur and Nathaniel Beverly Tucker, of Virginia. Troup was in the forefront as a political leader in Georgia while the tariff issue was being so hotly discussed in South Carolina. Upshur was a judge and served as United States secretary of the navy under President Tyler, but his reputation in later generations has resulted mainly from his *Brief Inquiry into the True Nature and Character of Our Federal Government*, a work published anonymously in 1840 as a review of Justice Joseph Story's *Commentaries on the Constitution of the United*

---

[45] See Jesse T. Carpenter, *The South as a Conscious Minority, 1789-1861* (New York, 1930), pp. 140-41.

States (1833). Nathaniel Beverly Tucker, a son of St. George Tucker, who had discussed the nature of federal systems earlier in the nineteenth century in an appendix to his edition of Blackstone's *Commentaries,* served for a time as a teacher of law in The College of William and Mary and published in 1845 a series of lectures on government. In these lectures, he set forth his views on the nature and character of the American union.

Troup did not treat state nullification of federal measures as a constitutional and peaceful process.[46] Yet he appears not to have doubted that each of the states in the union had a right under divine and natural law to take what action it deemed to be necessary to protect its independence and safeguard the interests of its citizens. As Governor of Georgia, he defied the executive branch of the central government by refusing to respect its policy in reference to lands occupied by the Creek Indians.[47] Replying to an invitation extended to him to attend a states' rights meeting in Columbia, South Carolina, in 1832, he wrote: "Whatever the people of South Carolina in convention shall resolve for their safety, interest and happiness, will be right, and none will have the right to question it." He added that the people of South Carolina could throw off the government of the union whenever their safety, interest and happiness required such action.[48]

Troup insisted that the central government of the United States was "a government of opinion, of consent, of voluntary association."[49] It had no constitutional right to coerce a member of the union into obedience to its measures. A state might indeed be guilty of violating its contractual

[46] George M. Troup, *Letter to a Gentleman in Georgia, on the Rights of the States and the Origin and Powers of the Federal Government* (Milledgeville, 1834), pp. 2-3.
[47] See *State Documents on Federal Relations,* ed. H. V. Ames (Philadelphia, 1911), pp. 113 ff.
[48] George M. Troup, *Letter to the Committee of Invitation to Attend the Columbia Dinner,* September 21, 1830 (Milledgeville, 1830?).
[49] *Idem.*

obligations to its sister states; but any damages resulting from such violation were matters to be settled by the states, without any interference from the central government.[50] Like the South Carolina supporters of nullification, Troup defined sovereignty in absolutist terms. He wrote:

This sovereignty, wherever it exists, is omnipotent; it is the same in one independent community as another, and is insusceptible of division, of increase, or diminution; it can only be destroyed, by destroying the community in which it exists. Constitutions, and governments are emanations from it, as light from the sun, which parts with it constantly, without itself being impaired, or wasted, or weakened. Hence it is, that it makes and unmakes at pleasure, and knows no superior but Divinity . . . [and] the law of right and justice. According to our theory and practice, the mode of action of this sovereign, is to form constitutions, which prescribe the rules for the conduct of the agent or servant called the government. If the sovereign is dissatisfied either with the rule or with the conduct of the agent, it can abolish or change it at pleasure. If it can abolish or change the rule, it can destroy the agent, because the rule is of higher power or authority.[51]

Sovereignty being indivisible, it was a mistake to assert that the states had "parted with many of their sovereign powers." The states had merely authorized their common agent to exercise some of these powers under prescribed rules and limitations.[52]

Troup conceded that the federal courts had "paramount jurisdiction" in "judicial cases," insisting that the jurisdiction of these courts did not extend to any "political controversies." He did not explain what "political controversies" were to be understood to include, any more than did the South Carolina nullifiers; but he at least considered them to include all controversies arising between the central government and the states or state governments over the extent of their re-

---

Troup, *To a Gentleman*, pp. 8-9, 15-16.
51 *Ibid.*, p. 4.   52 *Ibid.*, p. 5.

spective powers. If a controversy arose between the central government and the government of a state, it would be proper to seek a settlement by negotiation, for, as equals, the parties would have the right of equal participation in the settlement. The procedure for settlement was different for a controversy between the central government and a *state*, for here the relation between the parties was not that of equals but of creature and creator. As a creator and superior of the central government, the state must decide the controversy for itself.[53]

Upshur's *Brief Inquiry* has been referred to by a recent writer as perhaps the strongest historical analysis for the support of state sovereignty that has ever been written.[54] Yet there was certainly not much in Upshur's argument regarding the nature of the American union that was original and he apparently lacked the grasp of legal conceptions that characterized the thought of Calhoun. He made no use of the doctrine that sovereignty was indivisible. At the same time he contended that the states within the union were fully sovereign and that the central government was but their agent. Reviewing the evidence relating to the establishment of the union, he concluded that there was no support for Justice Story's argument that the people of the union were "one people." The basis of the central government was a compact among the states and they had a right to interpose their authority when this compact was violated.[55]

Just what was to be understood by state interposition was never made clear by Upshur. Clearly, he meant to argue that the central government had no right to coerce a state of the union which chose to oppose, on constitutional grounds, a federal legislative measure. He conceded that the states, in

---

[53] *Ibid.*, pp. 3-4.   [54] Carpenter, p. 203.
[55] [Abel P. Upshur], *A Brief Inquiry into the True Nature and Character of Our Federal Government: Being a Review of Judge Story's Commentaries on the Constitution of the United States* (Petersburg, 1840), pp. 90 ff.

adopting the federal Constitution, had made the United States Supreme Court the tribunal of last resort for certain classes of cases. These included cases between states, cases affecting ambassadors, other public ministers and consuls, and cases involving admiralty and maritime jurisdiction. But, according to Upshur, there were questions involving the powers of the central and state governments which could not assume a proper form for judicial inquiry. For such questions the states had provided no common umpire and as a consequence each state must decide the questions for itself.[56]

Upshur belonged to that school of nineteenth-century American thinkers who were extremely fearful of popular movements. He argued that people were too easily led by unprincipled demagogues and that the majority was all too ready to exercise oppressive rule over the minority. But he believed the federative form of political organization provided a corrective for these evils. Because of the diversity of American life, the majority of the people would inevitably have interests which were adverse to those of others in the community. But the checking and controlling power in the states, if exercised, would be an effective means of safeguarding minority rights.[57]

The lectures by Nathaniel Beverly Tucker added nothing to what had already been said many times regarding the nature of the American union. The views which they contained are discussed here primarily because they furnish an excellent example of the emotionalism that has so frequently accompanied assertions of the notion of complete state sovereignty and of the imagery that has been produced to convey this notion. Tucker was not so much concerned with specific remedies which a state might employ to redress an infringement of its rights; but he in effect argued that a state might do whatever it chose to do, regardless of the legal arrangements which it had established or entered into. Virginia might dissolve her "ancient incorporation," her people might disband or they might amalgamate themselves with another community by political fusion; but, as long as she retained her individuality, the right of a majority of her people to reform, alter or abolish any form of government that they had adopted or might adopt would remain *"indubitable, unalienable, indefeasible."*[58] Virginia was to be regarded not only "as one of the bright *stars* of our federal constellation, but as, in and of herself, a sun, sole and self-poised in the firmament of the commonwealth of nations."[59]

Like the South Carolina nullifiers, Tucker insisted that sovereignty in the American sense was in the people and not in government. Moreover, he argued that the idea of a people was not that of a "mere multitude of men," but that of men so associated as to form a body politic. The people of each state of the United States comprised a separate body politic, but there was no body politic of the United States as a whole. Although a number of bodies politic might combine for a common purpose, the several bodies politic thus associated formed but a league and did not create a new body politic compounded of the whole. Should Virginia abolish her state constitution, the majority of her people, acting according to the original terms of her social compact, might prescribe for the rest of the state's population what political form they chose. But if the Constitution of the United States were abolished, the authority of the central government could be restored only by the unanimous consent of the several states.[60]

The states of the union acted through the functionaries of the central and state governments, but they had surrendered none of their sovereignty to either of the two sets of functionaries. Those who talked of divided sovereignty

---

[58] Nathaniel Beverly Tucker, *Lectures on the Science of Government* (Philadelphia, 1845), pp. 377-78.
[59] *Ibid.*, p. 370.　　　　　　[60] *Ibid.*, pp. 380 ff.

talked of that which was absurd and could have no existence. There could be *"but one* supreme." There was "no
god but God."[61]

Conclusion

For the leaders of southern sectionalism, the federal form
in the United States became first and foremost a device for
affording protection to geographical minorities against majority domination. To make it serve this purpose to the full-
est possible extent no possible legal argument can be said to
have been neglected in the period between the passage by
Congress of the Tariff of 1828 and the Civil War. In fact,
by 1850 it had become practically impossible for anyone to
add to the legal arguments that already had been advanced.

The conclusions reached by the southern leaders as to
what would be legally proper and what would be legally im-
proper in the functioning of the American system were in
most instances inescapable if the original premises were
granted. Many of these premises could not be so easily attacked, since they consisted of legal conceptions that had
had a long history. Their validity could not be proven, but
neither could it be disproven. One could argue, however,
that leaving the states or their governments in a position
where they could constitutionally prevent the central government from exercising its delegated powers was inconsistent with the clearly expressed intention of those who had
been responsible for the founding of the union, even if it
was impossible to cite evidence that proved that the central
government had been intended to have a right to coerce
states. As a practical matter, the negative power which Calhoun and his followers claimed for the states and their governments seemed calculated to sap the central government
of all energy, if not to threaten the existence of the union.
To say that differences between the central government

[61] *Ibid.*, p. 388.

and the members of the union would be resolved by appeals
to the constitutional amending authority was to imply for
this authority a role which it could not possibly play. Regardless of how authoritative a constitutional amendment
might be, the difficulty of the amending process made it
unthinkable that the declaratory amendments contemplated
could meet the need for an umpire in the regular functioning
of the federal system.

America has chosen to be, in many respects, and to many purposes, a nation. . . .
—From Chief Justice John Marshall's opinion in the case of *Cohens* v. *Virginia*, 6 Wheaton 264, 414 (1821).

(6)

The Defense
of Central Authority

Divided Sovereignty

IT AT FIRST APPEARS A BIT CURIOUS THAT MOST OF THE states' rights advocates of the nineteenth century and most of those opposing them argued that the federal system of the United States exhibited a perfect dualism. The fact is, however, that the assumption of dualism was arrived at by different lines of reasoning, involving different conceptions of the state and its sovereignty. The more ardent states' rights advocates assumed that the central and state governments were equal agents of sovereign states, while their opponents commonly assumed that sovereignty was divided—divided between the central and state governments or divided between the people of each state and all the people of the United States.

Any number of assertions of the doctrine of divided sovereignty may be found in nineteenth-century literature, but the mention here of only two or three should suffice for illustration. Writing the opinion for the United States Supreme Court in the case of *McCulloch* v. *Maryland*, Chief Justice John Marshall stated that the "powers of sovereignty" were divided between the central and state governments. Each of the governments was sovereign with respect to the objects committed to it, but neither had any sovereignty over the objects committed to the others.[1] Another statement of the doctrine of divided sovereignty ap-

[1] 4 Wheaton 316, 410 (1819).

pears in the two-volume work by George Ticknor Curtis on the "origin, formation and adoption" of the United States Constitution. In this work, appearing in the 1850's, Curtis observed that the adoption of the Constitution had created "two supremes in the same country, operating upon the same individuals, and both possessed of the general attributes of sovereignty." He declared that there was nothing in the nature of "political sovereignty" to prevent its being distributed among different agents for different purposes. It was obvious that there might be "several enacting authorities," each "supreme over the particular subject committed to it by the fundamental arrangements of society."[2]

While arguing that "political sovereignty" had been divided between the central and state governments, Curtis went on to contend that there was a sovereignty superior to this which had been divided between the people of each of the several states and the people of the United States. He explained that

. . . while it is true that the people of each state constitute the sovereign power by which the rights and duties of its inhabitants not involved in the Constitution of the United States are to be exclusively governed, it is equally true that they do not constitute the whole of the sovereign power which governs those relations of its inhabitants that are committed to the national legislature. The framers of the Constitution resorted to an enactment of that instrument by the people of the United States, and employed language which speaks in their name, and for the express purpose, among other things, of bringing into action a national authority, on certain subjects. The organs of the general government, therefore, are not the agents of the separate will of the people of each state, for certain specified purposes, as its state government is the agent of their separate will for all other purposes; but they are the agents of the will of a collective people, of which the inhabitants of a state are only a part.[3]

[2] George Ticknor Curtis, *History of the Origin, Formation, and Adoption of the Constitution of the United States; with Notices of Its Principal Framers* (New York, 1858), II, 377-78.
[3] *Ibid.*, II, 380-81.

Another statement of the doctrine of divided sovereignty appears in a pamphlet published by the Harvard law professor Emory Washburn just at the close of the Civil War. In it Washburn, examining the right of a state to secede from the union, wrote:

> While I have attempted to analyze the Constitution, with a view to establish the fact of the sovereignty and supremacy of the United States, in respect to every subject matter delegated to its government, I would, with equal earnestness, insist that, as to all matters which were not provided for in the Constitution, the people of the states remained, after the taking effect of that instrument, to all intents and purposes, as sovereign and independent as they were before its adoption. Together the states with the United States form arcs of a circle in which neither occupies the same space as the other. . . . In this sense, Massachusetts is independent of Pennsylvania, New York of Ohio; and not only so, but each state is alike independent of the United States as it is of any of its sister states.[4]

Washburn saw no reason why the people of the states could not have merged themselves into one unit for certain purposes and yet have remained separate units for other purposes. He noted that in the past separate peoples had sometimes been joined in union for certain purposes while retaining the rights of local self-government.[5] The question that had been submitted to the "several peoples of the respective states" in 1787 had been "whether, as to certain subject matter of a purely national character they were willing to act as *one nation*."[6]

On the surface an assertion of the doctrine of divided sovereignty seems to be but a way of emphasizing an obvious fact: that the federalism decreed by the Constitution truly represents a middle position between the extremes of legal centralization on the one hand and legal decentralization on the other. This doctrine has been appealed to in opposing what appeared to be

---

[4] Emory Washburn, *Sovereignty in Its Bearing upon Secession and State Rights* (Cambridge, Mass., 1865), p. 33.
[5] *Ibid.*, pp. 16-17.   [6] *Ibid.*, p. 23.

centralizing tendencies as well as in opposing particularist arguments.[7] When appealed to for the latter purpose, the great difficulty is that those making the appeals have taken little note and have shown no particular grasp of the conception of sovereignty which they were actually opposing. Even after states' rights advocates began to make so much use of the premise that sovereignty is indivisible, it was unusual for one to attempt to demolish this premise, although many went on asserting emphatically that sovereignty in the American union was divided. Curtis attempted to refute the notion of indivisible sovereignty, but he appears not really to have grasped the meaning which the states' rights advocates of Calhoun's school associated with the term "sovereignty." They meant a power which was and could only be above law, while he was quite evidently writing about a power which could be and was under law.

Constitution versus Compact Among Sovereign States

One way of attacking directly the extreme states' rights position, of course, was to attack the view that the United States Constitution was a compact among sovereign states. For such an attack two separate approaches were possible. One might deny that the states in the union had ever been sovereign, as many of the proponents of strong union had done in 1787 and 1788. On the other hand, one might disregard this question but nevertheless insist, as did Patrick Henry and other opponents of the Constitution during the ratification controversy, that the act of adopting the Constitution was not an act of sovereign states. Both of these approaches were in some degree followed in replying to states' rights arguments between the adoption of the Constitution and the Civil War. In the case of *Penhallow* v. *Doane,* decided by the United States Supreme Court in 1795,

[7] Note, for example, President James Monroe's message of 1822 accompanying his veto of the Cumberland Road Bill. *Writings of James Monroe,* ed. S. M. Hamilton (New York and London, 1898-1903), VI, 222.

Justice William Paterson took the position that the states were not to be regarded as separately sovereign during the period of the Revolutionary War, although this certainly appears out of harmony with the position he had taken as a delegate in the Federal Convention of 1787. He explained in the Penhallow case that the people of the colonies had, in the War emergency, grown into a union, forming "one great political body, of which Congress was the directing principle and soul." Particularly in respect to "great national concerns," foreign powers had recognized the states to be sovereign, not individually but collectively.[8] This was the position that was later to be taken by Abraham Lincoln, who declared in his first inaugural address as President that the American union under the Constitution was much older than the Constitution itself, that it had been formed by articles of association in 1774.[9]

Writers of the first half of the nineteenth century who sought to answer the states' rights arguments did not as a rule concern themselves with the question of the status of the states before the adoption of the Constitution. After all, to deny that the states were fully sovereign under the Articles of Confederation was to remove a principal basis for distinguishing the union under the Constitution from the Confederation. It was commonly assumed that the Confederation had been weak because of state sovereignty and that the union under the Constitution had been made strong by eliminating state sovereignty, or a very considerable portion of it.

Conclusive evidence that the Constitution was not a compact among sovereign states was believed to be supplied by the document itself. Thus Justice Joseph Story, of the United States Supreme Court, declared in his *Commentaries on the Constitution:*

> . . . the difficulty in asserting it [the United States Constitution] to be a compact between the people of each state and all the

---

[8] 3 Dallas 54, 81.
[9] *Abraham Lincoln: His Speeches and Writings,* ed. Roy P. Basler (Cleveland and New York, 1946), p. 582.

people of the other states is, that the Constitution itself contains
no such expression, and no such designation of parties. We, "the
people of the United States, etc., do *ordain* and *establish* this *Constitution*," is the language; and not we, the people of each state,
do establish this *compact* between ourselves and the people of all
the other states. We are obliged to depart from the words of the
instrument to sustain the other interpretation; an interpretation
which can serve no better purpose than to confuse the mind in
relation to a subject otherwise clear.[10]

Similar language was used by Daniel Webster, who as a member of the United States Senate repeatedly made what were intended to be replies to the states' rights arguments.

. . . how can any man get over the words of the Constitution itself?—"We, the people of the United States do ordain and establish this Constitution." These words must cease to be a part of the
Constitution, they must be obliterated from the parchment on
which they are written, before any human ingenuity or human
argument can remove the popular basis on which that Constitution rests, and turn the instrument into a mere compact between
sovereign states.[11]

Webster thought it highly important that the Constitution
did not say that it was established by the people of the several
states, and he jumped to the conclusion that it "pronounced"
that it was established by the people of the United States in
the aggregate. He had no doubt, he said, that the people of the
several states when taken collectively constituted the people of
the United States, and it had been in their collective capacity,
as all the people of the United States, that they had established
the Constitution.[12]

Although it probably did not help his case any, Webster
argued that the Constitution was not a compact or contract in
any sense. It had originated as the result of an agreement among

[10] Joseph Story, *Commentaries on the Constitution of the United
States*, ed. Melville M. Bigelow, 5th ed. (Boston, 1895), I, 266.
[11] Daniel Webster, *Works*, 6th ed. (Boston, 1853), III, 477.
[12] *Ibid.*, III, 346.

the people, but once adopted it was not a mere agreement but a Constitution. When the people agreed to erect a government and actually erected it, their compact was executed and the end designed by it attained. Thenceforth the fruit of the agreement existed, but the agreement itself was merged in its own accomplishment, for there could no longer be a subsisting agreement or compact to form a constitution or government after that constitution or government had been actually formed and established.[13]

In interpreting the Preamble of the Constitution, Story and Webster, like Patrick Henry before them, appear to have relied almost entirely on intrinsic evidence. The assumption that the phrase "We the people of the United States" necessarily meant the people of the country taken collectively, without regard to state boundaries, could, as Calhoun showed, easily be countered if one only referred to the early drafts of the Preamble. In these drafts the people of each state had been mentioned, all of the states being enumerated by name.[14] The phrasing was changed after the Federal Constitutional Convention had decided to have the Constitution provide that it would come into effect in the ratifying states when nine states ratified it.

Nothing was more important to the argument that the Constitution was a compact among sovereign states than the fact that the ratification of the document was through the agency of conventions assembled in and consisting of delegates chosen in the various states. It was certainly not naive to think of these conventions as constituent bodies of the states, and not much was ever really done toward explaining why they should not be so regarded. John Marshall did attempt this explanation, but in doing so he attributed to such terms as "people," "state," and "government" meanings which he made no effort to defend but which conflicted with other meanings of these terms that were

---

[13] *Ibid.*, III, 468.
[14] See *Records of the Federal Convention of 1787*, ed. Max Farrand (New Haven, 1911), II, 177, 565.

in current use. His explanation was therefore immediately vulnerable to attack. The point that he intended to make was that the Constitution had been submitted for its adoption to conventions assembled in the states because no other satisfactory way of consulting the people had been available. Thus he wrote in his opinion in *McCulloch* v. *Maryland:*

> . . . the counsel for the State of Maryland have deemed it of some importance, in the construction of the Constitution, to consider that instrument not as emanating from the people, but as the act of sovereign and independent states. The powers of the general government, it has been said, are delegated by the states, who alone are truly sovereign; and must be exercised in subordination to the states, who alone possess supreme dominion.
>
> It would be difficult to sustain this proposition. The Convention which framed the Constitution was, indeed, elected by the state legislatures. But the instrument, when it came from their hands, was a mere proposal, without obligation, or pretentions to it. It was reported to the then existing Congress of the United States, with a request that it might "be submitted to a convention of delegates, chosen in each state, by the people thereof, under the recommendation of its legislature, for their assent and ratification." This mode of proceeding was adopted; and by the Convention, by Congress, and by the state legislatures, the instrument was submitted to the *people*. They acted upon it in the only manner in which they can act safely, effectively, and wisely, on such a subject, by assembling in convention. It is true, they assembled in their several states; and where else should they have assembled? No political dreamer was ever wild enough to think of breaking down the lines which separate the states, and of compounding the American people into one common mass. Of consequence, when they act, they act in their states. But the measures they adopt do not, on that account, cease to be the measures of the people themselves, or become the measures of the state governments.[15]

Of course, no states' rights advocate would have contended that measures adopted by the people ceased to be the people's measures and became measures of the state governments. The

[15] 4 Wheaton 402-03.

question which needed to be answered was whether the people were to be thought of as having acted on the Constitution as a number of separate corporate communities, or as one such community, or simply as individuals. Marshall did not answer this question, though presumably he did not think of the people as acting in any particular corporate capacity and tended to consider the term "state" as almost if not entirely synonymous with the term "government."

Central Paramountcy

Many if not most of those who in the nineteenth century spoke or wrote of divided sovereignty clearly visualized the American union as a system of co-ordinate governments. This notion was undoubtedly fostered by the assumption that it was an impartial tribunal to which had been committed the function of ultimately determining the boundary line between the governments. The tribunal which was understood to have this function—i.e., the United States Supreme Court—was a part of the central government, but it had been made largely independent of the political departments of that government even though the political departments had much to do with its composition and jurisdiction. Since the Court had been specifically called for by the United States Constitution, it was even possible to think of the states as having participated directly in its establishment. This reasoning was followed by Chief Justice Roger B. Taney, who both referred to the division of "sovereignty" and recognized the necessity of an impartial tribunal to determine the jurisdictional boundaries between the governments exercising sovereignty. He referred to the Supreme Court as having been created by the Constitution rather than by an act of Congress in order to secure the Court's impartiality.[16]

But it was not uncommon before the Civil War for one to assert that sovereignty was divided between the central and state governments and yet to say that the sovereignty pos-

[16] See *Ableman* v. *Booth*, 21 Howard 506, 521 (1858).

sessed by the central government was of a higher grade than that possessed by the states. No doubt this often merely reflected the assumption that a tribunal of the central government, whether impartial or not, had the constitutional right to pass finally upon the competence of both the central and the state governments. But other reasons were sometimes given for considering the sovereignty of the central government to be superior. Some of them were given in 1833 in the second edition of a book on principles of government by the Vermont lawyer Nathaniel Chipman. He insisted, for example, that the provisions of the Constitution requiring the central government to guarantee to states a republican form of government and to protect them against domestic violence involved obligations of a superior and not those of an equal or an ally. He explained that these obligations placed the central government "in the situation and grade . . . of a guardian and protector of the several states."[17] He also called attention to the provisions in the Constitution which specify that certain powers are to be exercised by the states only with the consent of Congress. He argued that sovereignty was not an indivisible essence, that the United States with its distribution of governmental powers on both a functional and a territorial basis furnished a "complete example" of divided sovereignty. Nevertheless, he insisted that the states' portion of sovereign power was "limited and adapted to the superior sovereignty of the national government."[18]

Another example of the tendency to think of sovereignty as being of two grades, one grade possessed by the central government and one by the states, is furnished in a book written by the Presbyterian clergyman George Junkin. Just prior to the outbreak of the Civil War Junkin held the position of president of Washington College in Lexington, Virginia, a position from which he felt compelled to resign because of his

[17] Nathaniel Chipman, *Principles of Government*, 2nd ed. (Burlington, 1833), p. 276.
[18] *Ibid.*, pp. 273-74.

lack of sympathy with the views of the secessionists. Sovereignty, defined as the governing authority in a state, he held to be not only divisible but "necessarily divided, wherever freedom dwells." The "idea of sovereignty being a unit, and a unit *sui generis,* incapable of division," belonged to "a newer philosophy." But in the United States all the "higher attributes of sovereignty" belonged to the central government.[19] At one place, Junkin wrote:

> We saw that sovereignty is an absolute unit only in the hand of God; that in human hands the distribution of ruling power is a necessity; consequently, that the lower functions are apportioned out to subordinate officers, and only the higher reserved to the king, president, governor, legislature, &c. So, in our Providence-invented system, in the states is deposited, by the people, to whom God gave the whole, a large and important part of the sovereignty, to be by them exercised for their particular and special benefit. These lower functions regard all the local interests of the people near home and within the sphere limited and bounded by the national Constitution. The general government includes all the higher functions of sovereignty which have been delegated to it by the people of the whole nation, to be exercised for the good of the whole. It is the grand depository of the supreme functions; the ponderous flywheel which regulates the movements of the whole system of machinery; the central sun, whose attractive force preserves the unity of all the surrounding planets, whilst its light guides them in the paths they pursue.[20]

Merely attributing to the central government a "superior sovereignty" could, of course, in no sense be regarded as meeting the states' rightist argument which assumed that ultimate sovereignty was the exclusive possession of a political community considered as distinct from its government and assumed further that there were many such communities within the American union. Noticeable in the three decades

[19] George Junkin, *Political Fallacies: An Examination of the False Assumptions and Refutation of the Sophistical Reasonings, Which Have Brought on This Civil War* (New York, 1863), pp. 46, 245.
[20] *Ibid.,* pp. 152-53.

immediately preceding the Civil War, however, is the gradual
development of the notion that the people of the United
States comprised a compact national community, that the
Constitution had originated from this community, and that
this community was now to be regarded as ultimately sovereign over any governments and over any other political
communities existent in the country. Nathan Dane, a prominent Massachusetts lawyer, argued in 1829 that "the *original*
sovereignty in the *whole* of the American people" was the
only real sovereignty in the country. This sovereignty, he
wrote, was limited only by the laws of God. The "original
sovereignty of the people of a state" was, on the other hand,
very much limited by the Constitution. When the people of
Massachusetts had adopted their state constitution, they had
"confessedly acted in subordination, as a part of the American people, as to the powers vested in the general government
by the whole people, or to be so vested."[21] While Justice
Story relied largely on intrinsic evidence afforded by the
Constitution in replying to states' rightist arguments, he accepted the premise that the people of the United States comprised a national community and argued that it was established principle that the majority within any such community
had the right to establish rules for governing the whole of
the community. He wrote:

> The truth is, that the majority of every organized society have
> always claimed and exercised the right to govern the whole of
> that society, in the manner pointed out by the fundamental laws
> which from time to time have existed in such society. Every rev-
> olution, at least when not produced by positive force, has been
> founded upon the authority of such majority. And the right re-
> sults from the very necessities of our nature; for universal con-
> sent can never be practically required or obtained. The minority
> are bound, whether they have assented or not; for the plain reason

[21] Nathan Dane, *A General Abridgement and Digest of American Law,
with Occasional Notes and Comments* (Boston, 1829), IX, 58, 64,
Appendix.

that opposite wills in the same society, on the same subjects, cannot prevail at the same time; and, as society is instituted for the
general safety and happiness, in a conflict of opinion the majority
must have a right to accomplish that object by the means which
they deem adequate for the end. . . . In a general sense the will
of the majority of the people is absolute and sovereign, limited
only by their means and power to make their will effectual.[22]

That the people of the United States comprised a national
community and that this community was paramount in
authority to all governments and to any other communities
within the country were argued by the Ohioan Edward D.
Mansfield, whose career included the practice of law, college
teaching, and newspaper editing. In his *Political Grammar of
the United States*, which went through two editions, one
appearing in 1834 and the other in 1851, he referred to the
people as "one nation, governing itself, by virtue of the
original, natural and inherent rights of man." The government of this nation was a government of laws which were
sustained by the "whole community."[23] Sovereignty, the
"highest power," was possessed by the people of the nation.
The states of the union were not sovereign, for sovereignty
was not possessed by a community, city, or state which
formed a part of another community or state and was represented in foreign relations through that other community or
state. To be sovereign a state must govern itself without any
dependence on another power.[24]

Whether or not this was to mean that the states were entirely subject to the will of the nation Mansfield did not
make clear, although he probably didn't intend to go that far.
He agreed that the term "sovereign" was, in some of its
"common acceptations," not an inappropriate term to use in
describing the legal status of the states and he compared the

[22] Story, I, 237-38.
[23] Edward D. Mansfield, *The Political Grammar of the United States*,
rev. ed. (Cincinnati, 1851), p. 192.
[24] *Ibid.*, p. 19.

control which states had over their domestic and "municipal" relations to an individual's control over his household affairs. Just as a man might be said to be perfectly sovereign in his own house when he was subject to the laws of society, so also the states, considered as composing a society, might be regarded as sovereign and independent in their domestic and "municipal" relations.[25]

The idea of a unified American national community fully sovereign within itself received its greatest emphasis before the Civil War in the writings of Francis Lieber, a German born and educated scholar who spent most of his life as a teacher of history and governmental subjects, first at South Carolina College and later at Columbia University. Like the South Carolina nullificationists, Lieber clearly distinguished state from government, and like them he defined sovereignty as the self-sufficient source of governmental power. A state was a social organism composed of people with jural relationships. It was not deliberately created but developed naturally, resulting from the nature of man.[26] Sovereignty was the "basis of all derived, vested, or delegated power, the source of all other political authority—itself without any source, imprescriptible in the nature of man." It consisted in the necessary existence of a state, and that right and power which "necessarily or naturally" flowed from it.[27] The idea that sovereignty could be delegated, or that governments were sovereign was a fallacy, for sovereignty inhered only in society and it never passed from society.

The assertion that society, or the people, divest themselves of sovereignty and delegate it to someone else, is as contradictory in itself, and can be as little imagined, as if we should force our minds to suppose the trees of a forest delegating one tree to be green for them, or to sprout in spring for them—nay more diffi-

---

[25] *Ibid.*, p. 38.
[26] Francis Lieber, *Manual of Political Ethics* (Pt. I, London: 1839; Pt. II, Boston: 1839), Pt. I, pp. 171, 256.
[27] *Ibid.*, Pt. I, pp. 231-32.

cult, because sovereignty and state are ideas essentially united, one being only the attribute of the other, as omniscience is of God.[28]

Government was merely the institutional framework through which a sovereign state functioned when the state itself did not choose to act directly.[29] If government were to be reckoned as sovereign, it would be necessary to admit the existence of two sovereign authorities, and this was absurd.[30] What was called a "division of sovereignty" could only mean a "division of power," for sovereignty was not capable of being divided.[31]

Of primary importance in cementing the bonds of nationhood were sociological forces, such as a common culture, a common language, and common interests.[32] Such forces had long been present among the people of the United States, and these people had actually been in the process of developing into a single national entity before the Constitution was adopted. The Continental Congresses and the union under the Articles of Confederation were to be regarded as outward evidences of a drawing together of the people into one nation.[33] The frame of government under the Constitution was justly called "a federal republic," but the Constitution was a "national law" which preceded "from the fullness of the national necessity, national consciousness and national will" and was "expressive of a national destiny." The general government under the Constitution "nationally" united a number of states "with the framework of local governments."[34]

Lieber is the one who did most before the Civil War to

[28] *Ibid.*, Pt. I, p. 234.   [29] *Ibid.*, Pt. I, p. 254.
[30] *Ibid.*, Pt. I, p. 255.
[31] Francis Lieber, *Civil Liberty and Self-government*, ed. Theodore D. Woolsey, 3rd ed. (Philadelphia, 1901), p. 152.
[32] Lieber, *Manual of Political Ethics*, Pt. I, p. 153. See also Lieber's *Two Lectures on the Constitution of the United States* (New York, 1861), pp. 16-17.
[33] See the *Two Lectures*, pp. 18 ff.; the *Manual of Political Ethics*, Pt. II, p. 522; and Lieber's *Fragments of Political Science on Nationalism and Internationalism* (New York, 1868), p. 13.
[34] Lieber, *Civil Liberty*, p. 258; and *Two Lectures*, p. 33.

counter the extreme states' rights arguments. This is not because he did anything to demonstrate the untenableness of the conceptions of state and sovereignty on which the arguments were based, for he himself made use of these same conceptions. What he contributed that might be regarded as an answer to the states' rights advocates was an interpretation of historical evidence which was wholly different from theirs and which yet could appear reasonable if one assumed that the institutions of a nation might take on a variety of separate forms, old forms giving way to new as the will of the nation changed. But Lieber had no better grounds for holding that the people of the United States constituted a nation and for attributing indivisible sovereignty to this entity than the states' rights advocates had for holding that the people constituted a number of separate states and for attributing indivisible sovereignty to these entities. The forces which were supposed to have made for national unity were not fundamentally different in character from forces pulling in the opposite direction—forces which had been responsible for the failure of the constitution-makers of 1787 to abandon completely the principle of a federal division of powers and which were even now responsible for the continued emphasis upon states' rights. It was only reasonable to regard the adoption of the United States Constitution as indicative of a general development in the direction of national unity; but it was still about as reasonable to argue that the Constitution had emanated from political communities which in many respects were quite separate and distinct from one another and which had jealously withheld powers which they did not consider it absolutely necessary to relinquish.

The Constitution, in all its provisions, looks to an indestructible union, composed of indestructible states.

—Opinion of the United States Supreme Court in the case of *Texas* v. *White*, 7 Wallace 700, 725 (1869).

The Commonwealth [a "state" of the United States] really exists only in its governmental organization, while the nation has a physical and an ethnical existence as well as a governmental. There is really no such thing as the people of a commonwealth, in a sound view of our political and social system; there is only the people of the nation resident within the commonwealth. The people is a national conception, and preserves its integrity against government only as nation. Blot out the national government, and you still have the nation physically and ethnically, which, by its own innate power, will restore its political organization; but blot out the government of the commonwealth, and you have a territory measured by the chain of the surveyor, with a population governed exclusively by the nation's organs, and restored to local self-government only by the nation's act.

—John W. Burgess, "The American Commonwealth," *Political Science Quarterly*, I (1886), 25.

The Post-Civil War Era

The "Indestructible" Union of "Indestructible" States

MOST OF THE THEORISTS OF THE POST-CIVIL WAR ERA attempting to explain the relationship between the two centers of power within the American union spoke in terms of the doctrine of "divided sovereignty." Although this doctrine has meant different things to different people, its most common meaning at this time appears to have been that the general and state governments had been permanently placed on a plane of equality with each other. In any event, this was a meaning given to the doctrine in decisions of the United States Supreme Court. In the case of *Texas* v. *White*, the first important case after the War involving the nature of the union, the Court laid down the dictum that the Constitution in all its provisions looked to an indestructible union composed of indestructible states. The Court in effect took the position that none of the thirteen original members of the union had ever been fully sovereign entities. The union had begun among the colonies; it had been declared by the Articles of Confederation of 1781 to be perpetual; and the Constitution had been ordained to make it a "more perfect" union. The act by which Texas' admission into the union had been consummated had been more than a compact, and it had been final, leaving no place for reconsideration or revocation except through revolution or the consent of the states. Yet the "perpetuity and indissolubility" of the union by no means implied the loss of distinct and individual existence or the right of self-government by the states. It might, said the Court, not unreasonably be said that the preservation of the states and the maintenance of their governments were as much within the design and care of the Constitution as the preservation of the union and the maintenance of the "national government."[1]

In later cases the Court indicated its acceptance of what the late Professor Edward S. Corwin, of Princeton University, labeled the doctrine of "dual federalism," i.e., the doctrine that the purpose and scope of the delegated powers of Congress are impliedly limited by the existence of the reserved powers of the states. The basic assumption here is that the reserved powers of the states are intended to be a fixed bundle of powers, subject to change only by formal constitutional amendment.[2] This is one of the principles of constitutional interpretation for which states' rights advocates had been contending, without, however, always being explicit on the point. As judicial doctrine the principle was not new, for it clearly influenced the Supreme Court during Roger B. Taney's term as. chief justice.[3]

Between 1865 and 1900, numerous attempts by state governments to regulate economic affairs were thwarted by decisions of the Court which declared that the state statutes in question represented attempts to interfere with Congress' power to regulate interstate and foreign commerce or that the statutes were forbidden by the due process clause of the Fourteenth Amendment. But the Court interpreted narrowly Congress' powers under the Fourteenth Amendment in respect to civil rights, mainly on the ground that a broader interpretation of these powers would permit invasion of the reserved rights of states and thus endanger the existence of the

---

[1] 7 Wallace 700, 725-26 (1869).
[2] See Edward S. Corwin, *The Twilight of the Supreme Court: A History of Our Constitutional Theory* (New Haven, 1934), Chap. I.
[3] *Ibid.*, pp. 11-12. For opinions of members of the Court illustrating acceptance of the principle during Chief Justice Taney's term see the *Passenger Cases,* 7 Howard 283 (1849).

federal system.[4] The same deference for states' rights and for
the future of the federal system was shown by the Court near
the end of the century in reference to Congress' power to
regulate interstate and foreign commerce. While the Court
held that Congress had the power to regulate the movement of
goods in interstate and foreign commerce, it took the position
that the manufacture of goods intended for this movement
was a local matter and thus subject to state regulation only.[5]

The doctrine that the federal Constitution had intended to
mark off two mutually independent and fixed spheres of power
—spheres that were to be changed only by formal constitutional amendment—appears not to have been seriously challenged in the late nineteenth century by any substantial portion of the legal profession. It is worthy of note that the
doctrine was accepted by Thomas M. Cooley, the author of
the well-known treatise on constitutional limitations on the
legislative powers of the states which first appeared in 1868—
a treatise described by Professor Corwin as the most influen-
tial work on American constitutional law ever published.[6]

Indivisible and Illimitable Sovereignty

Although the notion of divided sovereignty tended to
dominate the legal thought of the post-War years relating to
the American union, the number of writers supporting the
doctrine of an indivisible and illimitable sovereignty continued
to be large. Southern leaders, under the charge of war guilt
and, in some instances immediately after the Civil War under
formal charges of treason, insisted that this sovereignty was

[4] See the *Slaughter House Cases*, 16 Wallace 36 (1873), and the *Civil
Rights Cases*, 109 U.S. 3 (1883).
[5] *United States v. E. C. Knight Company*, 156 U.S. 1 (1895).
[6] See Thomas M. Cooley's *A Treatise on the Constitutional Limitations
Which Rest upon the Legislative Power of the States of the American
Union* (Boston, 1868), his *General Principles of Constitutional Law in
the United States of America*, ed. A. C. McLaughlin, 3rd ed. (Boston,
1898), pp. 106, 111, 161-62, and Edward S. Corwin, *Constitutional
Revolution, Ltd.* (Claremont, Calif., 1941), p. 87.

possessed separately by the states. Northerners at one time or another held it to be in almost every conceivable part of the union except in the states as separate entities. There is evidence that members of both groups did some consulting of foreign authors; but whatever aid was received from foreign authors, the views advanced by the two groups of Americans had in most cases already had a history in America.

Among the southern leaders who after the Civil War continued to argue for the proposition that sovereignty was possessed exclusively by the states were Bernard J. Sage, a former naval officer and foreign emissary of the southern Confederacy, and Alexander H. Stephens and Jefferson Davis, who had served respectively as the Confederacy's vice-president and president. Sage wrote:

> It will be seen that sovereignty dwells permanently down in the people of these organized communities, and does not, as some suppose, continually bob up and down with successive delegations and withdrawals of power, like the hammers of a piano, or the "merry dancers" of the Aurora Borealis. It is the soul of each commonwealth, that never leaves its tenement—the great inherent, inalienable, indivisible and illimitable right of supremacy—by virtue of which international conventions are made; agencies, governmental or other, constituted; powers delegated; and rights and privileges conferred.[7]

According to Sage, all that was read about "delegated sovereignty," "sovereign powers vested in the government," "surrendering essential parts of sovereignty," or "dividing sovereignty between the federal and state governments," was palpably absurd and the offspring of confusion in thought.[8] The existence of the "thirteen commonwealths" at the time the United States Constitution had been adopted had made the

[7] P. C. Centz, pseud. of Bernard J. Sage, *Davis and Lee: A Protest Against the Attempt of the Yankee Radicals to Have Them and the Other Confederate Chiefs Murdered: A Vindication of the Southern States, Citizens and Rights* (London, 1865), Preface.
[8] *Ibid.*, p. 45.

existence of a nation composed of the people of these commonwealths a legal impossibility.[9]

Sage pointed out that the word "federal" was derived from the word *foedus*, meaning "a league," and that the word "constitution" was derived from the word *constituo*, meaning "to constitute." Putting the two words together, he claimed that they meant a "league constituted, or a constituted league —*just exactly what sovereign states could and would make.*"[10]

Stephens summed up in detail the southern argument for the right of state secession in his two-volume work *A Constitutional View of the Late War Between the States.* He was later to be referred to by the nationalist John W. Burgess as a "fair-minded and conscientious man,"[11] and it is true that his work is far more moderate in tone than most of the polemical writings of the great sectional controversy, including both northern and southern writings. Stephens announced that he had never been an advocate of the doctrine of state nullification,[12] but he had no doubt that while a state might be obligated to respect decisions of the federal judiciary so long as it remained in the union, it also had a perfect right to leave the union. By appropriate quotations and citations from earlier states' rights theorists he supported the proposition that the states as members of the union were fully sovereign. For example, he quoted at length from Calhoun's speech of Febru-

---

[9] *Ibid.*, Preface.   [10] *Ibid.*, p. 42.

[11] See John W. Burgess, "The American Commonwealth: Changes in its Relation to the Nation," *Political Science Quarterly*, I (1886), 9-35, at p. 10.

[12] "Many who believed in the perfect right of secession, and looked upon that as the proper remedy in such cases of abuse of power as South Carolina complained of, were utterly opposed to nullification. How a state could remain in the union, with senators and representatives in Congress, and yet refuse obedience to the laws of Congress not set aside by the judiciary as unconstitutional, was, to this class, utterly incomprehensible. But the merits of this doctrine are not now before us. Suffice it to say that I was never an advocate of it." Alexander H. Stephens, *A Constitutional View of the Late War Between the States*, 2 vols. (Philadelphia, 1868, 1870), I, 421.

ary 26, 1833, in the United States Senate. This contained the passage from Tucker's *Blackstone* with Vattel's famous dictum that sovereign states might unite to form a confederacy without ceasing to be perfect states.[13]

Stephens, like Sage and earlier states' rights theorists, insisted that a clear distinction was to be made between sovereignty and the powers vested in governmental organs. The latter were divisible, but sovereignty was not.

> If I were to undertake to express my ideas of it in regular formula, I should say that sovereignty or paramount authority, in a proper political sense, is that inherent, absolute power of self-determination, in every distinct political body, existing by virtue of its own social forces, which, in pursuit of the well-being of its own organism, within the limitations of natural justice, cannot be rightfully interfered with by any other similar body, without its consent. With this explanation, . . . I have only to add, that sovereignty, as I understand it, is that innate attribute of the political body so possessing it, which corresponds with the *will* and power of self action in the personal body, and by its very nature is indivisible; just as much so as the *mind* is in the individual organism.[14]

Stephens indiscriminately used the terms "federal" and "confederate" in referring to the government established by the United States Constitution. He did not believe that this government fitted into the classification of political forms accepted by German writers. The American system, he said, was neither a *"Staatenbund"* exactly nor a *"Bundesstaat."* There was, to be sure, a generic likeness between this system and a *Staatenbund,* for its members, like those of a *Staatenbund,* collectively constituted a single international unit with respect to third parties and several international units with respect to each other. But there was a specific difference between the United States and a *Staatenbund,* for the central government of the United States enforced its laws on individuals without intermediate action on the part of the member states. In a *Staatenbund* the central government must act on individuals only with the sanction of

[13] *Ibid.,* I, 364.   [14] *Ibid.,* II, 22-23.

the member states. But while the American system differed in only a specific sense from a *Staatenbund*, it differed generically from a *Bundesstaat*, which was represented by German writers as being a union state, partly if not wholly sovereign. None of the sovereignty of the members of the American system had been surrendered or alienated, the system being in reality a "newly developed species of government of the German genus *Staatenbund*."[15]

Davis' work *The Rise and Fall of the Confederate Government* repeated the old basic arguments: The United States Constitution was a compact among states; sovereignty, the right of commanding in the last resort in civil society, was indivisible and was possessed by the people of each state; to the people of each state the central government was subordinate and responsible.[16] State secession, Davis explained, was the assertion of the "inalienable right" of a people to change their government whenever the government ceased to fulfill the purpose for which it was established. But it was neither revolution nor insurrection, for it consisted only in a state's action of withdrawing from a league.[17]

Outside the South sovereignty as indivisible and illimitable power was variously attributed to several bodies—to the states jointly; to the central unit because of its right to determine the competence of both itself and the member units or because of its own legislative powers; to the authority which amended the federal Constitution; to the people without reference to their identification with either the central or the member units; and to the people conceived of as constituting a nation.

The most prominent of the American writers who attributed sovereignty to the states of the American union as a joint possession were John C. Hurd, Boston lawyer, and Orestes A.

---

[15] *Ibid.*, II, 18-19.
[16] Jefferson Davis, *The Rise and Fall of the Confederate Government*, United Daughters of the Confederacy memorial edition (Richmond, 1938), I, 121, 133-34.
[17] *Ibid.*, I, 156.

Brownson, editor of *Brownson's Quarterly Review.* These two men probably owed something to the British jurist Sir John Austin. Austin had advanced the theory in 1832 that the sovereignty of the American union was "in the states' governments as forming one aggregate body," and his views along this line were known to Hurd when Hurd's later works appeared. Austin made the governments of the states of the union identical with the several bodies of citizens who chose the "ordinary legislatures." To these several governments taken in the aggregate the central government was to be regarded as "a subject minister." On the other hand, the state governments when taken singly were not sovereign, even over the people they governed.[18] These assumptions were apparently deduced from the purely mechanical features of the American system, the sovereignty of the aggregate being inferred from the role the state governments played in the constitutional amending process. Hurd and Brownson, on the other hand, emphasized the role of the states in the early development of the American union. The union, which Hurd called a "union-state," had come into existence in 1776 when the thirteen colonies had acted simultaneously in wresting sovereignty from the mother country. Since then the union had continued to exist as a result of the states' acting in concert. Sovereignty was the possession of the "political people," i.e., the holders of the elective franchise in the states. Only the "political people" of the union organized into states, said Hurd, had shown that will and force which were necessary to the possession of sovereignty.[19] Brownson distinguished between what he called the "providential constitution" of the

[18] John Austin, *The Province of Jurisprudence Determined* (London, 1832), pp. 257 ff.

[19] See John C. Hurd, *The Theory of Our National Existence, as Shown by the Action of the Government of the United States since 1861* (Boston, 1881), pp. 112, 325 ff.; John C. Hurd, *The Union-State: A Letter to our States-Rights Friend* (New York, 1890), pp. 8 ff., 82 ff., 98 ff.; and Orestes A. Brownson, *Works,* comp. Henry F. Brownson (Detroit, 1882-1907), XVII, 569, and XVIII, 565 ff.

United States and the written Constitution. The former had preceded the latter and had vested sovereignty in "the distinct people of the several states united."[20]

A clearly evident desire of Hurd and Brownson was to avoid the extremes of both centralization and decentralization and yet to give support to the state suicide theory advocated by Charles Sumner, who led the Senate's Radical Republicans in their effort to bring about a drastic "reconstruction" of the southern state governments. According to Sumner, these states had by their attempted secession reduced themselves to the status of territories under the complete governance of Congress. As measures in opposition to the Constitution and government of the United States, the ordinances of secession were void; but these ordinances had not been impotent in the southern states' work of self-destruction. Being civil societies these states might continue to exist, but they no longer existed as members of the union possessing the rights held by loyal states. Their constitutional governments had been vacated and thus the whole "rebel region" had lapsed under the exclusive jurisdiction of Congress and was in precisely the same situation as any other territory of the United States. The whole region was "*tabula rasa,* or a 'clean slate,'" where Congress, under the federal Constitution, might write laws.[21]

Brownson condemned secession as untenable, expressing at the same time his indebtedness to Hurd for having shown him

[20] Brownson, *Works,* XVII, 571, 591, and Orestes A. Brownson, *The American Republic: Its Constitution, Tendencies, and Destiny* (New York, 1866), pp. 222, 227 f.
[21] Charles Sumner, "Our Domestic Relations, or How to Treat the Rebel States," *Atlantic Monthly,* XII (Oct., 1863), 507-29, at pp. 519, 522, 524. The above views of Sumner harmonize with a set of resolutions introduced by him in the United States Senate in 1862. In the resolutions it was declared that a state's vote of secession when supported by force was treason and meant instant forfeiture of "all functions and powers essential to the continued existence of the state as a body politic." The states' territory fell under the exclusive jurisdiction of Congress. See Charles Sumner, *Complete Works,* statesman's ed. (Boston, 1900), VIII, 164.

that there was a middle ground between separate state sovereignty and "consolidation."[22] The two men contended that the states of the American union held sovereignty as a joint possession in virtue of their continued will to exercise it, and that in the absence of this will, a particular state would possess no sovereignty in any sense of the term. The absence of this will was manifested when a state attempted to leave the union. Declining to be sovereign in the only way it could be, the state ceased to be a state, its territory remaining under the sovereignty of the union, which became the exclusive possession of the states remaining in the union. Thus, by adopting ordinances of secession in 1860-1861, the southern states had committed state suicide and had *ipso facto* placed their territories under the common government of the states that remained members of the union. Said Hurd: The ordinances of secession left sovereignty "an undiminished unit, exclusively in the states continuously holding it by the fact of their voluntarily continuing in union; the territory and population of the refusing states remaining under the same sovereignty as before."[23]

The main line of argument of the American writers of the post–Civil War years who attributed sovereignty to the central unit while denying it altogether to the states had already been marked out by American nationalists of the pre-War era. However, some of the post-War American writers followed in part lines of argument suggested by German jurists, and some of them were clearly under the influence of the philosophy of Friedrich Hegel.

Alexander H. Stephens, as has been noted, distinguished the federal system under the United States Constitution from both

[22] Brownson, *Works*, XII, 579 ff.
[23] Hurd, *Theory of Our National Existence*, p. 145. For Brownson's views on the effect of the ordinances of secession on the legal status of the southern states see his *Works*, XVII, 228 ff., and his *American Republic*, pp. xii, 282 ff.

the German *Staatenbund* and the German *Bundesstaat*.[24] On the other hand, Theodore D. Woolsey, of Yale College, whose two-volume work entitled *Political Science* appeared in 1878, pronounced the distinction which the German writers drew between a *Staatenbund* and *Bundesstaat* to be a valuable one and classified the United States as a *Bundesstaat*.[25] His definition of a *Bundesstaat* was in keeping with the one generally accepted among the German jurists in the decade or so immediately following the creation of Bismarck's Reich, when sovereignty was being defined in Germany in rather precise Bodinian terms. A *Bundesstaat* was a state formed out of states or dependencies of another state or of other states. The creation of a *Bundesstaat* did not bring about a complete merger of the entities out of which it was formed, but there was now one sovereignty where previously there may have been several. There could not be two sovereigns, one without any international powers and without many properties essential to a true state, the other with these in full.[26] The members of the American union were not sovereign in any true sense, the "only true and eminent sovereignty" of the union being that of the central state.[27] Woolsey gave various reasons for considering the United States to be a true state. But presumably he accepted the German proposition that one essential characteristic of any truly sovereign state was its constitutional right to determine its own competence. In any event, he noted that the federal judges of the United States determined in the last resort the meaning of the federal Constitution.[28]

---

[24] Nineteenth-century German theories having to do with the *Staatenbund* and *Bundesstaat* have been analyzed in detail by Rupert Emerson in his *State and Sovereignty in Modern Germany* (New Haven, 1928). See especially Chap. III.
[25] Theodore D. Woolsey, *Political Science, or The State, Theoretically and Practically Considered* (New York, 1878), II, 169-70.
[26] *Ibid.*, II, 169, 173, 251.
[27] *Ibid.*, II, 251.
[28] *Ibid.*, II, 250, 252.

Woodrow Wilson followed the lead of the German jurists of the period in holding that sovereignty was at that point where the constitutional right existed to determine competence. On this ground he held that sovereignty in the American union was at the common center and labeled the United States a "federal state"—a term which by this time was in fairly common usage and which appears frequently to have been understood as the English equivalent of the German *Bundesstaat*.[29] In addition, Wilson adopted the German conception of the non-sovereign state. This conception, which is to be associated with Georg Meyer, Paul Laband, and Georg Jellinek, applied to the members of a *Bundesstaat* or federal state. Though what powers these entities had could be drawn from them by the central state in the exercise of its right to determine competence, the entities nevertheless possessed underived rights of rulership, the essential requirements of statehood. They were to be distinguished from other associations within their borders, for these associations derived whatever rights they had from higher authority.[30] With reference to the status of the members and the central unit of the American union, Wilson wrote, following closely the reasoning of Laband and Jellinek:

> They are still states, because their powers are original and inherent, not derivative; because their political rights are not also legal duties; and because they can apply to their commands the full imperative sanctions of law. . . . They have dominion; but it [the central state] has sovereignty. For with the federal state lie the highest powers of originative legal determination, the ultimate authority to warrant change and sanction jurisdiction.[31]

However, it is not to be assumed that the new federalist conceptions for which the German jurists were responsible were ever widely adopted in the United States. While Stephens re-

[29] Woodrow Wilson, *An Old Master and Other Political Essays* (New York, 1893), p. 93.
[30] See Emerson, pp. 101 ff.
[31] Wilson, p. 94.

jected the label *Bundesstaat* for the United States, others criticized the notion that the members of a federal system like the
United States or the German Reich were to be regarded as
true states. These others were, like Woolsey and Wilson,
scholars in the universities where the writings of the German
jurists were best known. The conception of the non-sovereign
state was attacked by both John W. Burgess and W. W.
Willoughby, professors of government at Columbia College
and Johns Hopkins University, respectively.

According to Burgess and Willoughby, it was inconsistent
to deny that a political entity was sovereign while attributing
to this same entity underived rights of rulership. As Burgess
expressed it, a power to command and compel obedience
which was "underived and independent" was itself sovereignty. If the sovereignty of a "federal system" was exclusively in the union, the union was the only real state; the only
distinction between the separate "states" and the municipalities within their borders was that while the municipalities
derived their authority from the "states" in a "positive and
definite manner," the "states" derived their power from the
union in a "permissive and general manner." For one to be
completely scientific in his nomenclature, he should give the
name "state" only to the union and find some other term to
designate its members. Americans, Burgess went on to point
out, already had a suitable title for these members in the term
"commonwealth," and Willoughby agreed with him.[32]

Not only did Burgess and Willoughby reject the conception
of the non-sovereign state, but they both questioned the current usage of the term "federal state." In effect they held
that the term too frequently suggested disunity, while the
entity to which it was accustomed to refer was characterized
by its unity. Willoughby explained:

[32] John W. Burgess, "Laband's Public Law of the German Empire," *Political Science Quarterly*, III (1888), 123-35, at pp. 128-29; and W. W.
Willoughby, *An Examination of the Nature of the State* (New York,
1896), pp. 244 ff.

Strictly speaking, the only correct manner in which the term may be used . . . is to designate a state in which a very considerable degree of administrative autonomy is given to the several districts into which the state's territory is divided: not a political type in which there are *imperia in imperio*. . . . The state is by nature a unity, and is characterized by the possession of a sovereign political will that is of necessity a unity.[33]

Both Burgess and Willoughby considered the United States to be a national state. Whether or not this state had come into existence at the time of the adoption of the Constitution was, according to Willoughby, a question that could not be answered by resort to historical evidence, for historical evidence clearly indicated both the existence and the absence of feelings of political unity. The national state was now simply a fact which had been established conclusively by the outcome of the Civil War.[34] Burgess, however, like Lieber, held that the people of the United States had comprised a unified national community even before the adoption of the Constitution. He even called the Continental Congress meeting in Philadelphia an assembly of "the nation's representatives." The then united people had been organized only in that Congress and through it they had asserted their sovereignty, the Congress becoming a successor to the British government. It had been the obligation of this Congress as a constituent body to frame a constitution for a permanent system of government, but, preoccupied with the war with England, it had delayed this matter until the states had usurped the powers of the nation, placing themselves upon ground that was "false to philosophy, false to history, and false to physical and ethical relations." They had been represented as sovereign and independent in the plan of government adopted in 1781, but the

---

[33] Willoughby, p. 243. For Burgess' comments on the use of the term "federal," see his *Political Science and Comparative Constitutional Law* (Boston, 1896), I, 79 ff., 165, and II, 7.
[34] Willoughby, pp. 266-67, 269, 273.

nation had reasserted its sovereignty when, later, the Constitution was framed.[35]

Burgess attacked the doctrine of the indestructibility of the states, confidently hoping that the "federal era" of the United States was already drawing to a close. He saw in recent constitutional changes strict limitations imposed by the nation on the powers of the "commonwealth governments" and he looked for the further diminution of these powers. It was, he declared, unmistakable that a stronger consciousness of nationality had taken hold of the whole people.[36]

Burgess' faith in the national state and his analysis of its development placed him in company with German philosophers of the school of Hegel to whom he had become indebted while a student at the University of Berlin. Like Hegel, he represented the national state as a culmination of an historical process which was both rational and purposeful.[37]

The assumption that the people of the United States comprised a corporate national community and that this community was to be regarded as supreme over all associations and governmental institutions within it appears repeatedly in other political writings of the last 35 years of the nineteenth century. It was, for example, a predominant theme in the writings of John Alexander Jameson, a Chicago judge, John N. Pomeroy, who served on law faculties in New York and California, and Elisha Mulford, an Episcopal clergyman in New Jersey. Jameson emphasized that the people of the United States constituted an indivisible nation and argued that this nation possessed the ultimate power denominated sovereignty. By the exercise of this power the nation had created the Confederation of 1781 and had later ordained and established the United States Constitution, "parcelling out

[35] Burgess, "The American Commonwealth," pp. 19-22.
[36] *Ibid.*, pp. 23 ff.
[37] See Bernard Edward Brown, *American Conservatives: The Political Thought of Francis Lieber and John W. Burgess* (New York, 1951), pp. 118, 123, 136, 172-73, 175.

anew and in different manner the powers it saw fit to grant at
all." It was now in the power of the people of the nation to
remodel or abolish the governments of both the states and the
union and even to wipe out the states as political associations.[38]
Pomeroy held it to be "demonstrable as a fact of history . . .
that the people of the United States . . . sprang into self-
existence as an organic political society possessing sovereignty." The member states of the union, he contended, were
in a position of permanent subordination. For the present they
had "perfect" rights within their sphere, but the people might,
by following the process of constitutional amendment which
they themselves had prescribed, completely abandon the
states or the idea of local self-government. Moreover, the
power to interpret the federal Constitution, the "organic law"
of the nation, must in the final analysis rest with the nation to
be exercised through its "imperial government."[39] Both Pomeroy and Jameson assumed that the people of the nation had an
obligation to respect established procedures for bringing about
constitutional changes, but Jameson noted that the established procedures were not enforcible except by "moral sanc-
tions."[40]

The influence of Hegel is particularly evident in the book
entitled *The Nation* by Mulford, who himself acknowledged
his indebtedness to the German philosopher. In it the "nation"
is declared to be the work of God in history.[41] The nation
might exist in some transient period through "confederate or
imperial forms," but the characteristic of these forms, if the
nation did not fail in its "integral organic and moral power,"

[38] John Alexander Jameson, *A Treatise on Constitutional Conventions:
Their History, Powers and Modes of Proceeding*, 4th ed. (Chicago,
1887), pp. 31, 54.
[39] John N. Pomeroy, *An Introduction to the Constitutional Law of the
United States*, ed. Edmund H. Bennett, 10th ed. (Boston and New York,
1888), pp. 31, 40, 74-75, 89-90, 103.
[40] Jameson, p. 31.
[41] Elisha Mulford, *The Nation: The Foundations of Civil Order and Political Life in the United States* (Boston, 1889), p. 358.

was lack of permanence.[42] The separate "societies or commonwealths" of the United States had no integral historical life and there was no separate historical aim that might be apprehended in them.[43] The real sovereignty was in the nation, the will of the "organic people" being prevalent through the whole.[44] The constitution of a nation ought to express the nation's continuous will, and if it failed to do so, it should be changed, regardless of whether or not it provided for its formal amendment. The "organic people" always had the right to remove obstacles to the nation's growth.[45]

Conclusion

One of the most significant aspects of American constitutional thought in the post–Civil War years is the continuing emphasis which it gave to the dualism between the central and state governments and to the duty of the federal courts to act as guardians of this dualism. Aside from this, the theorizing about the nature of the American union was but an expression of the emotionalism kindled by the War and an exercise in legal definition going far beyond any advantage to be gained from it once the question of the right of a state to secede from the union had been decided. Interest in the nature of sovereignty and in pinpointing its location in the union waned as the country got farther and farther away from the War and the issues which it involved. "State sovereignty" and "national sovereignty" were to survive to the twentieth century and continue to be used as symbols in rallying opposition to or support for federal legislative measures and federal court decisions; but sovereignty as illimitable power in the hands of some determinate superior had all but ceased to be appealed to by 1900. Since then it has not been invoked in explicit terms by any prominent American writer or political leader.

---

[42] *Ibid.*, pp. 352-53.   [43] *Ibid.*, p. 334.
[44] *Ibid.*, p. 302.   [45] *Ibid.*, pp. 151-52.

The question of the relation of the states to the federal government is the cardinal question of our constitutional system. . . . It cannot, indeed, be settled by the opinion of any one generation, because it is a question of growth, and every successive stage of our political and economic development gives it a new aspect, makes it a new question. The general lines of definition which were to run between the powers granted to Congress and the powers reserved to the states the makers of the Constitution were able to draw with their characteristic foresight and lucidity; but the subject-matter of that definition is constantly changing, for it is the life of the nation itself. . . . The old measures of the Constitution are every day to be filled with new grain as the varying crop of circumstances comes to maturity.

—Woodrow Wilson, *Constitutional Government in the United States* (New York, 1908), p. 173.

(8)

Twentieth-Century Trends

Federalism and Environmental Change

AN IDEA WHICH HAS GROWN IN THE TWENTIETH CENtury is that the jurisdictional boundaries between the central and state governments of the United States will and ought to change through new interpretations of the constitutional provisions by which they were established. Woodrow Wilson's view that they are to be determined anew by each new generation—that the federal Constitution is "a vehicle of life" whose spirit "is always the spirit of the age"[1]—was not unique even in the early decades of the century. It had the support then of a more general theory of jurisprudence—a theory which rejects the two ideas: that law is derived from fixed principles and that law changes only at irregular intervals and at the will of some determinate superior. Law is conceived to be an instrument of society which is regularly being shaped by judges as well as by legislative bodies to satisfy changing human demands. This "sociological theory" of jurisprudence (associated in its early history with former Justice Oliver Wendell Holmes of the United States Supreme Court and former Dean Roscoe Pound of the Harvard Law School[2]) has

[1] Woodrow Wilson, *Constitutional Government in the United States* (New York, 1908), p. 69.
[2] See Oliver Wendell Holmes, *The Common Law* (Boston, 1881), p. 1, 35-36; Holmes, "The Path of the Law," in *The Mind and Faith of Justice Holmes*, ed. Max Lerner (Boston, 1943), pp. 71-89, at p. 75; and Roscoe Pound, *Interpretations of Legal History* (Cambridge, Eng., 1930. First printed in 1923.), pp. 152 ff. The general trend in American legal

gained adherents as it has been necessary to deal through government action with problems of increasing population density, industrialization, and modern warfare.

Especially significant for federalism has been the fact that many of the new problems to be faced have been national in scope and yet have arisen in areas traditionally understood to be under state jurisdiction. This is well illustrated by the field of economic affairs. Before 1900 business enterprise was assumed to be primarily a matter for regulation by the state governments under the states' reserved powers. Congress attempted to deal with business monopoly by passing the Sherman Anti-Trust Act in 1890, but this was as far as it had ventured into the field of general economic regulation. To the state governments was left the responsibility for dealing with such matters as employer-employee relations and the buying and selling of corporate securities, insofar as these matters could legally be regulated at all. Yet the growth in size and number of private corporations posed difficulties which were beyond the state governments' reach. Only the central government could hope to deal effectively with those multifarious activities of corporations which transcended state boundaries. Even in agriculture, where much of the production remained in the hands of small operators, expanded markets made these operators dependent upon conditions which they and the state governments were powerless to control. If the farm population was to be protected from periodic price decline of farm commodities, the protection had to be provided by the central government.

The idea of a federal system with flexible boundaries which permit the shifting of power and responsibility from the member entities to the central establishment so that new conditions may be accommodated is one for which the general in-

interpretation in this century and its importance for federalism is discussed by Pound in an essay on "Law and Federal Government," in *Federalism as a Democratic Process* (New Brunswick, 1942), pp. 3-30.

tellectual environment of the United States in the twentieth century has not been wholly unprepared. The uncompromising provincialism which characterized American life in the early history of the country had by no means spent itself by 1900, notwithstanding the sentimental nationalism generated by the Civil War and reflected in such writings as those of John W. Burgess and Elisha Mulford. Nevertheless a remarkable change was soon to take place as a result of developments in transportation and communication. The following comment by United States Secretary of State Elihu Root in an address before the Pennsylvania Society in New York in 1906 doubtless contains more than just an element of truth:

Our whole life has swung away from the old state centers and is crystallizing about national centers. . . . The people move in great throngs to and fro from state to state and across states; the important news of each community is read at every breakfast table throughout the country; the interchange of thought and sentiment and information is universal; in the wide range of daily life and activity and interest the old lines between the states and the old barriers which kept the states as separate communities are completely lost from sight. The growth of national habits in the daily life of a homogeneous people keeps pace with the growth of national sentiment.[3]

There can be no question that Root exaggerated the unity which existed in 1906, for American life has continued to run in diverse channels. Wide variation between certain of the sections of the country in economic pursuits and general patterns of life has persisted. Moreover, sentimental attachment to local community may not today be regarded as a thing of the past, for it is still strong in the older sections. Yet state lines have meant progressively less to the majority of Ameri-

[3] Elihu Root, *Addresses on Government and Citizenship*, ed. Robert Bacon and James Brown Scott (Cambridge, Mass., 1916), pp. 363-70, at pp. 366-67.

cans as time has gone on and transportation and communication have improved.

The Continuing Emphasis on States' Rights

The American business community and the legal profession, including judges of the federal courts, were exceedingly slow to accept any theory which might result in a substantially more active central government. Traditional constitutional theory and the economic theory of laissez-faire were united in opposition to attempts by Congress to impose new economic regulations. The doctrine of states' rights was one of the principal weapons used in a struggle that was almost constant and was remarkably successful until the great economic depression of the 1930's, when it became clear that economic forces did not always obey the long-accepted laws of supply and demand. The history of the doctrine of states' rights in this century supports a comment by Professor Howard Lee McBain in 1927 that the doctrine is "a nomad, reviving whenever and dwelling wherever toes are trod upon or feelings severely ruffled by the exercise of federal power."[4] But it also seems clear that vigorous support for the doctrine in this century has come more frequently from economic groups opposing exercises of federal power than from any other source. Albert J. Beveridge wrote in 1907 that every corporation so big that its business was nation-wide was championing states' rights.[5] An address by William Gibbs McAdoo in 1926 was largely devoted to the zealousness with which states' rights were then being defended by persons associated with corporate enterprises. It was, he said, one of the tricks played on the past that the doctrine previously sponsored by Thomas Jefferson to protect the people from political tyranny should be invoked by monopolies to protect themselves from

---

[4] Howard Lee McBain, *The Living Constitution* (New York, 1927), p. 66.
[5] Albert J. Beveridge, "The Nation versus State's Rights," *Reader*, IX (1907), 357.

regulations adopted in the public interest.[6] An abundance of testimonials similar to these may be found for later years, along with supporting evidence.[7]

The United States Supreme Court did not turn a deaf ear to appeals to states' rights in the early decades of this century. The theory that the reserved powers of the states must be considered in determining the extent of the powers delegated to Congress had become a well established doctrine of the Court by the latter part of the nineteenth century. A few examples will suffice to illustrate that it continued to be accepted by the Court until well into the New Deal era.[8]

In 1918 in the case of *Hammer* v. *Dagenhart* the Court invalidated a federal statute prohibiting the shipment in interstate commerce of child-made goods on the ground that the statute represented an attempt to invade powers reserved to the states by the Tenth Amendment to the Constitution. Speaking through Justice William R. Day, the Court said:

> In interpreting the Constitution, it must never be forgotten that the nation is made up of states to which are intrusted the powers of local government. And to them and to the people the powers not expressly delegated to the national government are reserved. . . . The power of the states to regulate their purely internal affairs by such laws as seem wise to the local authority is inherent and has never been surrendered to the general government. . . . This Court has no more important function than that which devolves upon it the obligation to preserve inviolate the constitutional limitations upon the exercise of authority, federal and state, to the end that each may continue to discharge, harmoniously with the other, the duties intrusted to it by the Constitution. . . . The far-reaching result of upholding the act [of Congress] cannot be

[6] William Gibbs McAdoo, *State Rights and the Jeffersonian Idea*, 69th Congress, 1st Sess., Senate Doc. No. 121, p. 10.
[7] See especially Robert J. Harris, "States' Rights and Vested Interests," *Journal of Politics*, XV (1953), 457-71.
[8] For more detailed analyses of how the theory was applied by the Court in cases coming before it in the early decades of this century, see Edward S. Corwin, *The Twilight of the Supreme Court* (New Haven, 1934), pp. 26 ff., and Harris, pp. 462 ff.

more plainly indicated than by pointing out that if Congress can thus regulate matters intrusted to local authority by prohibition of the movement of commodities in interstate commerce, all freedom of commerce will be at an end, and the power of the states over local matters may be eliminated, and thus our system of government be practically destroyed. . . .[9]

While in *Hammer* v. *Dagenhart*, the Tenth Amendment was invoked as a limitation on the power of Congress over interstate commerce, in *United States* v. *Butler*, decided in 1936, the same Amendment was invoked as a limitation on Congress' power to tax and spend for the general welfare. In this case, the act of Congress in question imposed a tax on the processing of farm commodities; the proceeds were to be used for paying benefits to farmers who agreed to curtail production of their crops in accordance with a general plan of crop reduction to be administered by the federal Department of Agriculture. The processing tax held by the Court to be unconstitutional on the ground that it was a part of a general scheme of federal regulation of agriculture which represented an attempt by the central government to encroach on the reserved rights of the states.[10]

The same concern for states' rights was shown by the Court in the case of *A. L. A. Schechter Poultry Corporation* v. *United States*, decided in 1935,[11] and in the case of *Carter* v. *Carter Coal Company*, decided in 1936.[12] In these cases the Court denied that Congress' power to regulate interstate and foreign commerce included the right to regulate local business practices and working conditions in industry and mining, holding that such matters were local in character and emphasizing, in the Carter case, the importance of preserving the "fixed balance intended by the Constitution" to exist between the central and state governments. It had been the intention of the Constitution's framers to carve from the general mass

---

[9] 247 U.S. 251, 275-76.
[11] 295 U.S. 495.

[10] 297 U.S. 1, 68.
[12] 298 U.S. 238.

of state powers such portions as it was thought wise to vest in the central government, leaving the states "supreme" as to all powers reserved to them. To avoid uncertainty as to what was taken and what was left, the national powers of legislation had been "enumerated" rather than "aggregated," with the result that what was not embraced by the enumeration remained vested in the states without change or impairment.[13]

However, even before the end of 1936, the Supreme Court vacillated a great deal in the emphasis it gave to states' rights. In many of the cases which it decided before this time it sustained use by Congress of its power over interstate commerce to reach subjects which had formerly been regulated by the state governments under their police powers. It upheld as a valid use of the commerce power a federal statute prohibiting the sending of lottery tickets through the channels of interstate commerce,[14] federal regulation of railroad rates between points within the same state,[15] and a federal statute making it a crime to drive across a state line an automobile which was known by its driver to have been stolen.[16] In 1920 the Court upheld the use by the central government of its treaty-making power to regulate the killing of migratory birds after two federal district courts had held that this subject was local in character and therefore not under the delegated powers of Congress.[17] In 1936 the Court made it plain that it did not consider the reserved powers of the states as constituting an implied limitation on the central government's powers in foreign affairs. According to the Court, the powers in this field had passed directly from the British Crown to the American union at the latter's inception; they were not powers that had once been possessed by the state governments and later granted to

[13] 298 U.S. 294.
[14] *Champion* v. *Ames,* 188 U.S. 321 (1903).
[15] *The Shreveport Case,* 234 U.S. 342 (1914).
[16] *Brooks* v. *United States,* 267 U.S. 432 (1925).
[17] *Missouri* v. *Holland,* 252 U.S. 416. The cases in the federal district courts were *United States* v. *Shauver,* 214 Fed. 154 (1914) and *United States* v. *McCullagh,* 221 Fed. 288 (1915).

the United States by the Constitution. Speaking through Justice George Sutherland, the Court declared that the powers "to declare and wage war, to conclude peace, to make treaties, to maintain diplomatic relations with other sovereignties, if they had never been mentioned in the Constitution, would have vested in the federal government as necessary concomitants of sovereignty."[18]

Finally, between 1936 and 1942, a great change occurred in the Court's position regarding Congress' power to legislate in purely domestic matters. This half decade began with bitter criticism of the Court and an elaborate though unsuccessful plan of the central government's executive branch for the Court's reorganization. Notwithstanding the position it had taken in the Butler case regarding the use by Congress of its taxing and spending powers, the Court in 1937 upheld use of these powers for inaugurating a vast social security plan manifestly designed to induce states to adopt social security plans of their own to be administered under the general supervision of a federal Social Security Board.[19] In the same year, it abandoned its earlier doctrine that Congress' power over commerce did not extend to manufacturing activities, now holding that Congress might regulate employer-employee relations in manufacturing plants where employer-employee strife might be expected to burden or obstruct interstate and foreign commerce.[20] In *United States* v. *Darby*, decided in 1941, the Court formally rejected the theory that the Tenth Amendment placed on the central government limitations which did not exist from the moment the Constitution was adopted. That

[18] *United States* v. *Curtiss-Wright Export Corporation*, 299 U.S. 304, 316-18.

[19] *Steward Machine Company* v. *Davis*, 301 U.S. 548; *Helvering* v. *Davis*, 301 U.S. 619.

[20] *National Labor Relations Board* v. *Jones and Laughlin Steel Corporation*, 301 U.S. 1; *National Labor Relations Board* v. *Fruehauf Trailer Company*, 301 U.S. 49; *National Labor Relations Board* v. *Friedman-Harry Marks Clothing Company*, 301 U.S. 58; *Washington, Virginia and Maryland Coach Company* v. *National Labor Relations Board*, 301 U.S. 142.

Amendment, the Court said, "states but a truism that all is retained which has not been surrendered." There was "nothing in the history of the Amendment's adoption to suggest that it was more than declaratory of the relationship between the national and state governments as it had been established by the Constitution before the Amendment or that its purpose was other than to allay fears that the new national government might seek to exercise powers not granted, and that the states might not be able to exercise fully their reserved power."[21] The Court sustained in the Darby case Congressional regulation of the wages and hours of employees engaged in the production of commodities for interstate and foreign commerce, overruling its earlier decision in *Hammer* v. *Dagenhart*.

The decisions of the Supreme Court between 1936 and 1942 indeed mark a turning point in the history of the Court, for it has not since then returned to the theory that the reserved powers of the states are to be taken into account in determining the extent of the powers vested in the central government. Not only has Congress been permitted to make provisions for social security and regulate employer-employee relations and working conditions in industry, but it has also been permitted to adopt measures dealing with numerous other subjects which were formerly held not to be included within the scope of its delegated power. These measures have included extensive codes regulating public utilities and the buying and selling of corporate securities. They have also included elaborate programs for the development of adequate housing facilities and for the production, storage, and marketing of farm commodities. Yet if the doctrine of states' rights has ceased to influence the Supreme Court, there has been no noticeable lessening of the role of this doctrine in American political controversy. It has continued to be resorted to by various groups in opposing new federal economic controls and expansions in federal programs in the fields of health and welfare.[22] It has played a

---

[21] 312 U.S. 100, 123-24.   [22] See Harris, pp. 66 ff.

significant role in the politics of the South in the last quarter century as the dominant white majority of this section has reacted to the rise of the Negro race in social and economic status and in political influence. White political leaders of the South have used it in protesting against, and in some cases in efforts to justify resistance to, federal court decisions which invalidated state statutes and local practices found by the federal courts to discriminate against Negroes in violation of the civil rights clauses of the federal Constitution. They have also used it in fighting proposals for federal legislative measures for the enforcement of civil rights in the field of race relations.

In the first half of the twentieth century explicit statements of the states' rights doctrine did not ordinarily go beyond the proposition that the central government is obligated to avoid encroachments on powers reserved to the states by the Tenth Amendment.[23] But the doctrine's more revolutionary nineteenth-century version began to be revived in the South in the 1950's in response to the decision of the United States Supreme Court in *Brown* v. *Board of Education of Topeka*. In this case segregation of the races in state schools was declared a violation of the clause in the Fourteenth Amendment which prohibits a state from denying to any person within its

[23] Exceptions include some writings supporting the argument that the southern states had had a right to withdraw from the American union in 1860 and 1861, when they organized the southern Confederacy. See, for examples, Eugene B. Gary, "The Right of Secession," *Lawyer and Banker*, IV (1911), 197-211; Gary, "The Constitutional Right of Secession," *Central Law Journal*, LXXVI (1913), 165-75; and Forest G. Cooper, "The Constitutional and Legal Right of the Southern States to Secede in 1861," *Lawyer and Banker*, VI (1913), 225-32. During the era of national prohibition, it was sometimes argued that the rights of the states placed limits on the extent to which the federal Constitution could be changed by formal amendment. For example, see Archibald E. Stevenson, *States' Rights and National Prohibition* (New York, 1927). In this work Connecticut, which had failed to ratify the Eighteenth (prohibition) Amendment, was urged to adopt a resolution declaring that Amendment void insofar as it purported to give the central government control over intrastate business. The author argued that Congress and the legislatures of three-fourths of the states could not legally amend the Constitution at the expense of state sovereignty. See p. 130.

jurisdiction the equal protection of the laws.[24] When this decision began to be put into effect by lower federal court decrees, as directed by the Supreme Court, southern state legislatures, responding to popular demand to keep the public schools racially segregated, adopted a series of "interposition" resolutions.[25] Most of them accepted as fact the theory that the federal Constitution is a compact among states and made this the basis for assuming that a state had the right to challenge the validity of the Supreme Court's decision. The legislatures of Alabama, Florida, Georgia, Louisiana, Mississippi, and Virginia went on to allege in their resolutions that a case of contested power had arisen between the Supreme Court and their respective states. This case of contested power was to be settled, not by the Supreme Court, but by a constitutional amendment agreed to by at least three-fourths of the states comprising the union. The legislatures of Alabama and Mississippi stipulated that the Court's decision in the Brown case would be considered without legal effect within their states' boundaries until the case of contested power was settled.

The "interposition" resolutions were soon followed by a large number of statutes and other official acts in the southern states to circumvent the Court's decision or insure a maximum of delay in its implementation. In Arkansas the governor used military force to prevent the carrying out of a federal court-approved plan for racial integration of a public school in the city of Little Rock. In Louisiana the governor and legislature took special action to prevent the enforcement of lower fed-

24 347 U.S. 483 (1954).
25 "Interposition" resolutions for all of the former members of the southern Confederacy, except North Carolina and Texas, are printed in *Race Relations Law Reporter* (Nashville: Vanderbilt University Law School), I (1956), 437-47 (Alabama, Georgia, Mississippi, South Carolina, Virginia), 591-92 (Arkansas), 753-55 (Louisiana), 948-53 (Florida); II (1957), 228-30 (Tennessee), 481-83 (Tennessee), 707-10 (Florida). The "interposition" resolution in Arkansas was adopted by popular referendum, along with a state constitutional amendment directing the state's legislature to oppose the Supreme Court's decision in the Brown case. *Ibid.*, I, 1116-17.

eral court decrees for racial integration of public schools in the city of New Orleans. In an "interposition act" of the legislature the decrees were pronounced "null, void and of no effect" within the state,[26] while in subsequent acts the legislature sought to take over from the Orleans Parish School Board and superintendent administration of the city's public school system.[27] The governor of Mississippi, in a series of moves, sought to prevent enforcement of a federal court order for integration of one of the state's universities, going so far as to have himself chosen as the university's registrar and subsequently refusing admission to a Negro student. Much the same thing occurred in Alabama, where the governor stood in the doorway of a state university building to deny entrance to Negro students in defiance of a federal court order.

Responsibility for the delay which has occurred in the implementation of the Brown case decision in many parts of the South is unquestionably to be attributed in no small measure to the official acts of resistance and to sporadic acts of violence on the part of local white citizens against families of Negro students seeking to enroll in schools designated for white students under the states' segregation laws. Nevertheless, by the end of 1963 racially integrated schools were being operated by every southern state. The militant resistance in Arkansas, Louisiana, Mississippi, and Alabama was put down by the central government by display of its own armed might, the relevant court orders being enforced by the use either of federal marshals or of federal troops. Meanwhile the federal courts had occasion in two cases to dispose of the question whether a state or its officials might refuse to obey a federal court order as a matter of constitutional right.

The first of these cases was *Cooper* v. *Aaron*, decided in 1958,[28] in which the Supreme Court was called upon to re-

---

[26] *Ibid.*, V (1960), 1177-82.   [27] *Ibid.*, V, 1191-93, 1202-05.
[28] 358 U.S. 1.

spond to a petition by the School Board and superintendent of Little Rock for permission to postpone the carrying out of the school integration plan for that city. The reason given for postponement was that local animosities and violence made it impossible to maintain a sound educational program at the affected school. The Court denied this petition on the finding that the local difficulties cited were directly traceable to actions of the governor and legislature in their official capacities. Although it accepted without reservation the claim of the Board and superintendent that they acted in good faith, it held that this good faith could not be admitted as a legal excuse in implementing constitutional rights of individuals when their vindication was rendered difficult or impossible by actions of other state functionaries. Upon taking this position, the Court proceeded to answer the premise on which it found these actions to be based, namely, that the legislature and governor were not bound by the decision of 1954 in the Brown case. The Court reasserted the historic doctrine that the federal judiciary is supreme in the exposition of the federal Constitution, quoting appropriate passages from Chief Justice Marshall's opinions in *Marbury* v. *Madison* (1803)[29] and *United States* v. *Peters* (1809).[30] In addition it called attention to the supremacy clause of Article VI of the Constitution and to the oath taken by state legislators and executive officials, pursuant to this Article, to support the Constitution.

The second of the two cases dealing with the right of a state or of its officials to disobey a federal court order is that of *Bush* v. *Orleans Parish School Board*, decided in 1960.[31] In this case a three-judge federal district court panel rejected a petition to delay enforcement of an injunctive order of this court forbidding the Louisiana legislature and state and local officials from carrying into effect the legislative measures which were intended to keep the state's schools racially segre-

[29] 1 Cranch 137.   [30] 5 Cranch 115.
[31] 188 Fed. Supp. 916.

gated. The argument for delay in the enforcement of the order was that Louisiana by its "interposition act" had legally
interposed its authority to arrest implementation of the Brown
case decision until such time as the question of the validity of
this decision might be settled by an amendment to the federal
Constitution. The Court rejected this argument. Interposition,
said the Court, was not a constitutional doctrine but "defiance hidden under the cloak of apparent legitimacy." There
was nothing in provisions for amending the Constitution
which suggested that what was authoritatively declared to be
law ceased to be law while a proposal for an amendment was
pending or that non-ratification of the proposal altered the
Constitution or any decision rendered under it.[32]

An effort by counsel in this case to secure from the United
States Supreme Court a reversal of the lower court's ruling
was to no avail. In a *per curiam* announcement of December 12, 1960,[33] the Supreme Court denied motions for stay of
the ruling until an appeal could be prepared, terming as "without substance" the argument that Louisiana had interposed its
authority in the field of public education. Later the ruling was
affirmed by the Supreme Court.[34]

The decisions in the cases of *Cooper* v. *Aaron* and *Bush* v.
Orleans Parish School Board and the demonstrated readiness
of the central executive branch to back up federal court orders
by the use of force would, when taken together, seem to be
enough to discourage future overt acts of state interposition
or state nullification. But the doctrine of states' rights—which
began as a doctrine of the rights of the American colonies and
has had a continuous history since the colonial era—will
doubtless survive in some form for a long time to come, even
if the state governments should in the meantime become mere
administrative agencies of the central government. The notion that the federal Constitution originated as a compact

[32] 188 Fed. Supp. 926.   [33] 364 U.S. 500 (1960).
[34] 366 U.S. 212 (1961).

among states—which since 1789 has so frequently served to strengthen the states' rights doctrine and thus keep it alive— is by no means confined today to staunch defenders of the *status quo* in federal-state relations. As suggested by a British student of American government, it probably has roots deep in the political subconsciousness of most Americans.[35] In 1946 United States Supreme Court Justice William O. Douglas, whose constitutional interpretations have usually supported the trend toward federal centralization, asserted in a dissenting opinion that the federal Constitution was "a compact between sovereigns," obviously intending the term "sovereigns" to refer to states.[36] In 1957 President Eisenhower, who should be classified as a moderate where federal-state relations are concerned, stated in an address before the American Conference of Governors convened at Williamsburg, Virginia, that the central government was "not the parent, but the creature of the states, acting together."[37]

One can make a strong case for the proposition that the leading framers of the Constitution intended final interpretation of the document to rest with the federal judiciary and against any assumption that they thought of the document as falling under the strict rules of interpretation that are applicable to private contracts or to treaties between nations. But whether or not the Constitution originated as a compact among states is at bottom a question of semantics which is not likely ever to be given a definitive answer. All depends on the meaning which is given to the term "state," and the meaning which is given to the term "people of the United States" as used in the Preamble to the Constitution. Did the people who, as the Preamble declares, ordained and established the Constitution do so as a number of separate political communities to be known as states, as Madison contended in

---

[35] D. W. Brogan, *The Crisis of American Federalism* (Glasgow, 1944), p. 13 and note.
[36] *New York* v. *United States*, 326 U.S. 572, at p. 595.
[37] *New York Times*, June 25, 1957, p. 16.

the *Federalist* and in his Report of 1800 to the Virginia legislature? Or, are we to think of these people as having acted in some other capacity, reserving the term "state" for established governmental organs? On this matter there will doubtless continue to be different opinions.

The Maintenance of Federalism

Arguments protesting federal judicial invasion of state rights in civil rights cases tend to give the impression that court decisions in such cases often threaten the capacity of the American federal system to survive. On the contrary, although the decisions may limit the states' freedom of action, they do not transfer power from the state governments to the central government. The rights of individuals, protected by the federal Constitution against governmental interference, are not precisely the same for both state and federal levels; but generally it holds true that the Constitution's civil rights clauses mark off an area which neither the central government nor the state governments are free to enter. More significant than federal court decisions invalidating state statutes in civil rights cases, at least from the standpoint of the future of American federalism, is the lessening of judicial restraints on Congress as it acts to expand the powers and activities of the central government. The question is whether this expansion will eventually be carried to the point where the central government will possess all powers permitted to government by the Constitution. Some of those who have observed the centralizing trend of the last several decades have apparently concluded that federalism has in fact all but ceased to exist as a vital principle of American government.[38] Others have implicitly assumed that the principle will not survive if its survival is left

[38] See, for example, the comments by the Washington correspondent Roscoe Drummond at a panel discussion on the topic, "Are We Maintaining Our Federal System?" *State Government*, XXII, No. 1 (special supplement, January, 1949), 1 ff.

to depend primarily on restraints imposed by the central legislative and executive branches on themselves.[39]

Obviously the activities of the central government have vastly expanded since the New Deal era. But there is another side to the picture. State activities have also expanded during the same period. The difference is that their activities have not expanded at so accelerated a rate as have those of the central government. It has been found that central and state governments can act concurrently in vast areas without necessarily interfering with one another. An increase in activities at the center does not result in a limitation on the states' power to act except where state statutes are found by the federal courts to interfere with the implementation of measures adopted at the central level. It is significant that the number of cases in which the federal courts have actually invalidated state statutes on the ground that they interfered with implementation of the central government's measures have not been particularly numerous in the last several decades.[40]

To assume that the situation could change radically under the impact of new centripetal pressures would of course be only reasonable. Yet we have no real cause to assume that Congress or the central executive branch will be disposed in the foreseeable future to regard the federal boundaries as nonexistent, however indistinct these boundaries may have become. Recent appeals to the doctrine of states' rights have certainly not always been to no avail when they have been made in opposition to new federal legislative proposals. Con-

[39] See, for example, comments by United States Senator John W. Bricker. *Ibid.*, p. 13.

[40] Cases in which interference was found to exist and the state statutes in question were therefore invalidated include *Hines* v. *Davidowitz*, 312 U.S. 52 (1941), involving registration of aliens; *Rice* v. *Santa Fe Elevator Corporation*, 331 U.S. 218 (1947), involving regulation of warehouses engaged in storage of grain for interstate and foreign commerce; *Railway Employes' Department*, *A.F.L.* v. *Hanson*, 351 U.S. 225 (1956), involving labor relations of interstate carriers; and *Pennsylvania* v. *Nelson*, 350 U.S. 497 (1956), involving regulation of subversive activities.

gress, in particular, has shown a high degree of responsiveness to such appeals, either out of deference to genuine local interests and the principle of federalism or out of deference to large national interest groups which for tactical purposes go to the defense of states' rights. This indeed holds true for some subjects which have been held by the federal courts to fall within the range of Congress' powers, as is well illustrated by what has happened in the case of the business of insurance. This business, traditionally regulated and taxed by the state governments, was in 1944 held by the United States Supreme Court to fall under Congress' power to regulate interstate and foreign commerce.[41] But before a year had passed Congress, reacting to claims that the sphere of the states' reserved powers was being invaded, had adopted a self-denying ordinance nullifying for the time being, at least for all practical purposes, the Court's decision.[42] Declaring that the continued regulation and taxation by the state governments of the insurance business was in the public interest, Congress stipulated that silence on its part was not to be construed to impose any barrier to state regulation or taxation. Although the decision of the Supreme Court had made existing federal anti-trust legislation applicable to the insurance business, Congress suspended application of the legislation to such business for a period of approximately three years, at the end of which time the legislation would apply to the business only to the extent that it was not regulated by state law. Another case in point is that involving ownership and control over the lands submerged under waters adjacent to the coasts of the United States. When oil was discovered off the shores of California, Louisiana, and Texas, these states claimed ownership of the lands containing the oil deposits on the ground that the lands were within their historic boundaries. This claim was denied by the United States

[41] *United States* v. *South-Eastern Underwriters Association*, 322 U.S. 533 (1944).
[42] 59 *United States Statutes-at-Large* 33 (1945).

Supreme Court in decisions handed down in 1947 and 1950, the Court taking the position that the central government had paramount rights in the marginal sea and that an incident to these rights was full dominion over the lands covered by the water area.[43] The three states immediately involved and representatives of oil companies to which leases had been granted by the state governments for extractive operations soon began a movement to have Congress nullify the effectiveness of the Court's decision—a movement that was not long in winning support from public officials and private organizations in states which had no coastal borders. A bill passed by Congress in 1952 to accomplish the objective of this movement was vetoed by President Truman; but the question of ownership and control of the submerged lands almost immediately became an issue in the presidential election campaign of that year, the Republican Party giving its support to the proposal to turn the lands over to the states. The issue was finally disposed of by an Act of Congress in 1953 which was approved by President Eisenhower.[44] This Act defines the boundaries of the various states in the union and assigns to the states title to any undersea lands within these boundaries. The boundaries as defined by the Act are for the most part the boundaries which the states had when they became members of the union, although they are not permitted to extend from the coastline more than three geographical miles into the Pacific and Atlantic Oceans or more than three marine leagues into the Gulf of Mexico.

As we consider the ultimate effect of the lessening of judicial restraints on the central government, we should not forget the remaining checks on excessive and unconstitutional use of power which are built into that government's structure. Not the least among these checks are those which result from the

---

[43] *United States* v. *California,* 332 U.S. 19 (1947); *United States* v. *Louisiana,* 339 U.S. 699 (1950); *United States* v. *Texas,* 339 U.S. 707 (1950).
[44] 67 *United States Statutes-at-Large* 29 (1953).

role of the state governments in the composition of the central legislative and executive branches.[45] By constitutional provision the seats in Congress and presidential electors are still allotted to states. In the Senate representation is based on the principle of state equality, and, while in the House of Representatives it is based on population, each state is guaranteed at least one House member. The Seventeenth Amendment to the Constitution took from the state legislatures the right to choose United States Senators and vested it in the people; but the legislatures still have the right to determine voting qualifications for the choice of senators and representatives, subject to constitutional amendments which prohibit voting qualifications that are based on race, color, or sex. The number of presidential electors allotted to a state is the same as the number of senators and representatives which the state has in Congress, with the result that each state has at least three presidential electors. The state legislatures have the right to determine the manner in which the electors are chosen and have in fact vested this right in the same voters that choose the members of Congress.

The central government under the Constitution is by no means in the same category as the central government under the Articles of 1781. But neither is it in a class of governments whose inherent tendency is toward aggrandizement. There is some truth in the statement that Congress is composed of "local politicians," a number of whom achieve the status of national statesmen.[46] The presidency, because of the

[45] This subject is treated in some detail by Herbert Wechler in a chapter entitled "The Political Safeguards of Federalism: The Role of the States in the Composition and Selection of the National Government," in *Federalism Mature and Emergent*, ed. Arthur W. Macmahon (New York, 1955), pp. 97-114. A more general discussion of the checks and balances in the American federal system that may serve to keep the governments comprising it in proper bounds and responsible is included in William Anderson's *The Nation and the States, Rivals or Partners?* (Minneapolis, 1955), pp. 131-34.

[46] M. J. C. Vile, *The Structure of American Federalism* (London, 1961), p. 90.

larger constituency on which it depends, can be expected to reflect more often than Congress great national interests; but no presidential candidate who hopes to win in an election can afford to ignore local interests in states in which the outcome of contests for electoral votes is in doubt.[47]

The assumption that checks on the abuse of power which are built into the structure of the central government are being nullified by the existence of some large party combination has been fairly common. Calhoun, as we have seen, was by no means unaware of the role which had been given the state governments in the composition of the central legislative and executive branches; it served as the foundation for his claim that the central government had been based on the principle of a concurrent majority. But he held that this principle was being undermined by the development of the party system, and especially by a party combination concentrated in the northern section of the country.[48] The truth is, however, that none of the major American political parties has ever been a highly disciplined combination capable of dominating national policy over a considerable period of time. Their history seems clearly to bear out Madison's views as expressed in the tenth number of the *Federalist*. He was convinced that the diversity of interests to be found in a large country like the United States would make highly improbable the emergence of a numerical majority capable of exercising oppressive rule. For this reason he did not consider the powers contemplated for the central government to involve a serious risk for minorities or for the general public interest.[49] Although the United States has grown in unity in this century, apparently too much diversity still exists for the present major political parties to

[47] See Wechsler, pp. 105-08.
[48] *Supra*, Chap. 5, pp. 131-32.
[49] The *Federalist*, ed. E. G. Bourne (Washington and London, 1901), I, No. 10, 69-70. The validity of Madison's views as illustrated by the history of American political parties is discussed by Arthur N. Holcombe in his *Our More Perfect Union* (Cambridge, Mass., 1950), pp. 107-08, 145-47.

achieve any substantial degree of cohesiveness and yet remain major parties. Each of them is composed of groups with widely varying interests and sentiments. In organization they are decentralized to the point that they are really federations of self-sustaining state and local party organizations.[50] Before one of them could be in a position, after success in a national election, to nullify the checks built into the structure of the central government a substantial change would need to take place in its general character. Such a change does not appear to be in prospect for the immediate future.

Finally, the state governments by positive acts of their own may divert pressure from the central government for regulatory measures and services and thus limit its alleged infringement upon state jurisdiction. This point is emphasized by Elihu Root's address of 1906, a part of which is quoted on page 199. After observing that the people of the United States would have the governmental controls which they needed and thought just from either the central or state level of government, he commented:

> The true and only way to preserve state authority is to be found in the awakened conscience of the states, their broadened views and higher standard of responsibility to the general public; in effective legislation by the states, in conformity to the general moral sense of the country; and in the vigorous exercise for the general public good of that state authority which is to be preserved.[51]

We begin to perceive another of the major causes of the expansion in the central government's activities when we reflect on the slowness with which many of the state governments have acted in such fields as health, welfare, and educa-

[50] See V. O. Key, Jr., *Politics, Parties and Pressure Groups*, 4th ed. (New York, 1958), pp. 240-41, 361, and David B. Truman, "Federalism and the Party System," in *Federalism Mature and Emergent*, pp. 115-36, at pp. 116 ff.

[51] Root, p. 370. Similar views were expressed by Root in 1909 in an address before the New York legislature accepting election by the legislature to the United States Senate. *Ibid.*, pp. 247-55, at p. 252.

tion, and their failure in a number of instances to act in these fields until stimulated to do so by federal grants-in-aid— grants, albeit, which are usually accompanied by the condition that the aided activities must be administered in accordance with standards determined by federal agencies. In the last decade and a half, state governments have been repeatedly ac- cused of having done too little on their own initiative toward meeting legitimate demands for action on their part, particu- larly in these fields.[52] Yet it can be said that they have been less guilty of neglecting important governmental functions in recent years than they were in the early decades of this cen- tury.[53] This is evidenced by the large increase in the number of their activities and in the size of their budgets, after due allowance is made for what could be expected in view of the population increase and for the fact that many of the newer state governmental activities are actually financed largely by federal grants.[54] What the state governments will do in the future toward meeting their responsibilities will doubtless de- pend primarily on the quality of their executive leadership, the degree of administrative efficiency which they maintain, and the make-up of their legislative bodies—whether represen- tation in many of these bodies will disproportionately favor rural sections, as it has for a long period of time, or will be apportioned so as to reflect the interests and needs of the citi- zens at large. To one who would like to see more active state governments the outlook may not be especially en-

[52] For illustrations see the comments by former Senator Bricker of Ohio and former Governor William P. Lane of Maryland in "Are We Main- taining Our Federal System?" pp. 13, 18, and Robert S. Rankin, "The Impact of Civil Rights upon Twentieth-Century Federalism," Univer- sity of Illinois *Bulletin,* LX, No. 87 (May, 1963), 22.

[53] This opinion is supported by Leonard D. White in his *The States and the Nation* (Baton Rouge, 1953), p. 50.

[54] Although federal grants-in-aid to state and local governments amounted to approximately $6.4 billion in 1960, they still amounted to only a little over ten per cent of the total of state and local govern- mental expenditures for that year. See Council of State Governments, *The Book of the States,* XIV (Chicago, 1962-63), 213-77.

couraging; but at least it is not cause for complete discouragement. The state governments have made significant improvements in their administrative establishments in the course of this century,[55] and, while they have been exceedingly slow to reapportion their legislative bodies as population density has shifted from one section to another, progress toward equitable apportionment is being made. The decision of the United States Supreme Court in 1962 that apportionment of state legislative seats may violate the equal protection clause of the federal Constitution's Fourteenth Amendment and may because of this be a subject for review by the federal courts seems but to presage a far-reaching change in the character of many of the state legislatures.[56]

The sweep of events in this century and the general character of American industrial society would make it naive to assume that there will be a wholesale reversal of the trend toward governmental centralization. Problems which were once local but have become national in scope are not to be expected suddenly to become local again. But the areas in which the state governments may act effectively are still of substantial proportions and will doubtless continue to be so for a long time to come. In these areas at least the state governments have an opportunity to advance the welfare of their own citizens and in doing so contribute to their own preservation and the preservation of the American federal system.

[55] See White, pp. 50 f.
[56] See *Baker* v. *Carr*, 369 U.S. 186 (1962), and Rankin, p. 20.

Index